# The best of
# London

## THE CITY'S **ALL-TIME GREATS** AND **BEST-KEPT SECRETS**

Recommended by Londoners

Edited by Holly Ivins

The Best of London. The city's all-time greats and best-kept secrets
This first edition published in 2012 by
Crimson Publishing Ltd
Westminster House
Kew Road
Richmond
Surrey
TW9 2ND

Edited by Holly Ivins

**British Library Cataloguing in Publication Data**
A catalogue record for this book is available from the British Library.

ISBN 978 1 78059 119 3

Typeset by IDSUK (DataConnection) Ltd
Printed and bound in Singapore by Craft Print International Ltd

# Contents

3

# Picture Credits

28°–50° Wine Workshop and Kitchen p.32; Adam C Cresswell p.71 left; Ade Rowbotham - aderowbotham.com p.87 right; Agnieszka Wala p.25; Alan Lamb p.31 bottom left; Alan Stanton, flickr.com/photos/alanstanton p.92 left; Alys Tomlinson/University of the Arts London p.94; Andrew Firth p.63 right; Andrew M Whitman p.81; Andrew Smallwood p.26; Anne Marie Briscombe and The Royal Parks p.79 top left & right, p.88 top left; Anthony Falla p.47 right; Anthropologie p.52 right; Ben Bristow p.47 left; Bill Roy p.46 left; Byron p.39; Caroline Purday/TRAID p.48 left; Carolyn Gyseman p.69; Caronte Luciano p.68 right; Cassandra Martin p.77; Charlie Crowhurst/Corbis p.86 right; Chet DeFonso p.10 right; Cinnamon Club p.36; Cintia Rezende p.11 top; Comedy Carnival p.65; Cynthia Lopez p.48 right; Daniel Leach p.92 right; Daphne Chong p.85 top left; David Coyle: www.loupeview.com p.85 bottom left; David Sinclair p.63 left; Dee Dee Lim p.61 right; Dorin Odiatiu p.29 bottom; Erin Rose Foley p.15 top; Ewan Munro p.12; Ewart F Tearle p.58; p.76; flickr.com/irishtravel p.45; p.82; Gerhard Jenne p.8 right; Giles Barnard and The Royal Parks p.6; p.79 bottom left; p.87 left; p.89; Graham Coleman p.11 bottom; Heatheronhertravels.com p.18 bottom; Historic Royal Palaces p.21 left; Honeyjam Toys p.43; Howard Shooter and Euphorium p.8 left; Hunterian Museum at The Royal College of Surgeons p.59; Indusfoto Ltd and The Royal Parks p.83; p.88 bottom left & right; p.93; Jackie Hewitt p.56; Jacky Jordan, Hull p.84; Jennifer DeGuzman-Rolfe of Jen's Just Desserts p.34 left; Jo Folkes p.68 left; Justin Grunau p.60; Kay Mumme p.86 left; Keith van Loen p.22 right; Kevin Hoyt p.61 left; KOKO London p.62; Lexi Cinema p.74; Linard Brüngger p.44 right; Linus Chen p.30; Lisa van Gorder p.29 top; London Beatles Store p.46 right; London Duck Tours p.90 left; Loz Pycock, flickr.com/blahflowers p.85 right; Lucas Dillon/Mark Rigney/BLITZ p.49; Mahiki p.75; manna cuisine, manna LLP p.23 left; Mick Cole p.80; Noble Inns Ltd p.41; oliverbonas.com p.42; Paul Evans p.15 bottom; Paul Winch-Furness p.57; Peer Lindgreen p.52 left; Petya Velcheva p.70; Phil White p.7 top; p.10 left; Pollards Hill Cyclists p.18 top; Raziq, flickr.com/rmy101 p.64 left; Richard Kaszeta p.35; Rob Fuller p.91 left; Robbie Phelan p.64 right; Robert Diplock p.14; Robert Kidman p.7 top; Roelof Bakker p.90 right; Rough Trade p.53; S. Watson p.31 right; Sanderson Hotel p.20; Simon Jacobs p.71 right; Simon Rawles for Borough Market p.51 right; Simona Belotti p.17 left; Soho house group, Chris Tubbs p.21 right; Spherical Images p.28; Stefan Galler p.91 right; Stephanie Sadler p.31 top left; Susan Brandt p.13 right; Suzannah Banton p.50; The London Canal Museum, www.canalmuseum.org.uk p.73; The National Portrait Gallery p.66, p.67; The Old Operating Theatre Museum p.72 left; The Olde Bank of England p.13 left; The Star at Night p.17 right; The Zetter Townhouse p.16; UCL Grant Museum/Matt Clayton p.72 right; Under the Greenwood Tree p.55 left; Winston Lee p.37; Yeukyi Li p.38; Yu-Kuang Chou from http://scrambledimages.com/ p.24.

# Introduction

When I first moved to London, I quickly learned that London life operates on recommendations. The city is just too big; there's too much choice and too many tourists to stick to the obvious and simply visit chains or names that you recognise. I was soon asking, 'Where should I go for dinner with an old university friend?', 'Where should I take my mum for a treat when she visits this weekend?' or 'Where can I go to enjoy the sunshine after work?' The responses I got meant that I soon built up a little library of favourite places and reliable options. After living here for a while I found myself passing on my tips to other people and realised that rather than just keeping my favourites to my group of friends and colleagues we could widen our circle and put together as many recommendations as we could to create the ultimate list of London tips.

So that's what this book is: recommendations, tips and pointers from a range of people on what they consider to be the best of London. It's the city's best-kept secrets and great features, all recommended by real people, and we hope that it will help us all to live London life to the full.

In putting together this book, we heard from:

- Blue Badge Tour Guides
- bloggers
- students
- young professionals
- professionals who aren't as young as they used to be
- a range of nationalities (American, Australian, Welsh, Scottish, English and a few in between)
- parents with young children
- parents with older children
- a US Army Ranger
- people who have always lived here
- people who have just moved here
- and people who now consider London home.

Primrose Hill

Using all of the nominations we received, we've put together a whole host of tips, pointers and recommendations and grouped them into different categories:

- food and drink
- shopping
- art and culture
- open spaces and sport.

Throughout the book you'll also find some fun lists with tips on things to do with kids and our pick of the best things to do for free in the city, as well as ways to experience the unique aspects London offers, such as places or events where you can see the Queen.

Working on this book has shown me how much I still need to discover about London and how many amazing places there are to eat, shop and explore. Whether you're new to the city, you're just visiting, or you feel that you know the streets like the back of your hand, hopefully this book will help you to discover some new favourites to add to your prized list of what you consider to be the best of London.

Films at Somerset House

## A final note

All the recommendations in this book are impartial and honest. There is no advertising or sponsorship in this book, so you can be assured that everything included comes from a real person giving their candid opinion.

At the time of going to print we made every effort to ensure that all the information is accurate and that all the places we have recommended are still open for business. However, prices can change, shops can move and restaurants can close, so please do check in advance before heading out to try any of our recommendations. That aside, read on to discover the wealth of personal favourites, cult classics and one-off marvels in the city that so many have come to love.

The Ship at night

If you think there's anything we've missed or you'd like to suggest any of your top London finds, please email us at bestoflondon@crimsonpublishing.co.uk.

# Food and Drink

With such a multicultural population and a huge number of people looking for something exciting to eat and drink, London offers an incredible range of cuisines, with a wonderful variety of restaurants and bars. Whether you're looking for somewhere a little bit different for a special occasion, the perfect pub or a traditional café, you're sure to find the perfect place from our pick of the best food and drink.

## *Brilliant*
# Bakeries

### Euphorium
*Islington, N1 1RQ*
This bakery offers varied and unusual cake choices and lots of different types of bread (such as walnut, olive, tomato) in a lovely, light and airy café with big wooden chairs and tables.

### Princi
*Soho, W1F 0UT*
The cakes on offer beneath the counter scream indulgence, but as Princi is open until midnight on weekdays, it's the perfect stop-off for a strawberry slice, or maybe even a chocolate and amaretto brownie, on the way to the theatre.

### Gail's Artisan Bakery
*Hampstead, NW3 1QH and other locations*
Gail's is the place to go for freshly baked homemade bread. It also does brilliant coffee, pastries and cakes. Gail's bread is sold in Waitrose and Harvey Nichols but for a really cosy experience you need to visit one of the cafés.

### Konditor & Cook
*Waterloo, SE1 8TW and other locations*

A chain that does some of the best brownies ever! There are several varieties, they let you try samples (try not to stuff yourself!) and they do wonderful cakes for special occasions.

### Primrose Bakery
*Primrose Hill, NW1 8LD and Covent Garden, WC2E 7PB*
Cupcake heaven! Primrose has a huge choice of flavours that will leave you drooling. There are only a small number of tables but the cafés have a lovely homely feel.

# Top Places for Brunch

### Hudson's Wine Bar
*Putney, SW15 1EX*
One of the best breakfast menus, from American pancakes to eggs Benedict and even a breakfast burger! The menu has a great variety of dishes and there's always a great atmosphere, with families, young professionals and even the occasional rowing team refuelling after a gruelling session at the nearby rowing clubs. The Bloody Marys are excellent, as is the Buck's Fizz, and the coffee is great. Tell them it's your birthday and they will decorate the table for you!

### The Diner
*Camden, NW1 7BY and other locations*
Kitsch 1950s American décor, with the buzz of Camden from the rooftop terrace, fat fries and shakes, together with a menu offering everything from huevos rancheros and English breakfasts to corn dogs and guacamole, combine to make this the best place around for brunch after a night on the town. A superbly spicy Bloody Mary also helps to wash away the sins from the night before.

### Konnigans
*Wandsworth Town, SW18 1SS*
Great for eggs Benedict, a fry-up, pastries or muesli. Perfect for a lazy Sunday.

### The English Restaurant
*Spitalfields, E1 6AG*
This family-owned restaurant aims to deliver traditional English cooking, making it the place to go for breakfast classics like kippers, Cumberland sausage sandwich and bubble and squeak with fried egg. Breakfast is served until 1pm at the weekend.

### Kensington Square Kitchen
*Kensington Square, W8 5EP*
The Kensington Square Kitchen offers a varied menu in a pleasant setting, with toned-down décor overlooking one of London's oldest squares. Choose from scrambled eggs with sourdough to an egg and bacon burger accompanied by a choice from the morning cocktail selection to while away the morning.

Mexican breakfast at Hudson's

# Perfect Pubs for a
# Summer's Evening

### The Ship
*Wandsworth, SW18 1TB*
Great boozer with a large deck area overlooking the river. There's often a barbecue going and there's a great atmosphere when the sun's out.

### The Woolpack
*London Bridge, SE1 3UB*
A good range of drinks and a decent menu make this a great place to hang out in the sun after work.

### The Mayflower
*Rotherhithe, SE16 4NF*
Located just by the station on the river, the pub takes its name from the fact that the *Mayflower* was moored here before its eventual journey to the New World. Quality ales and an amazing patio located right on the river make this a pub with a lovely atmosphere and incredible views of the river.

### The Palm Tree
*Mile End, E3 5BH*
It can be a bit tricky to find this place in the middle of Mile End Park, but it's well worth the effort. Located on the banks of Regent's Canal, it's a wonderful place to enjoy a sunny pint sitting on the grass. The interior also deserves a mention: the gold walls, ancient cash register and red velvet bar add to the charm, making The Palm Tree a real East End experience.

### The Anchor
*South Bank, SE1 9EF*
Great historic pub set on the South Bank of the Thames with great views over the city and its own fish and chip shop. Sit outside and watch the lights go down over the city.

### The Flask
*Highgate Village, N6 6BU*
Well-organised outdoor space with comfortable seating and great food. So tranquil, it seems as though you're miles away from London.

### The White Swan
*Twickenham, TW1 3DN*
A great pub on the river, with a nice courtyard where you can enjoy your drink while watching rowers go past. They also have barbecues in the summer.

The Ship

## Captain Kidd
*Wapping, E1W 2NE*
A large beer garden facing the Thames and, as it's a Sam Smith's pub, reasonable prices.

## The Pub on the Park
*Hackney, E8 3PE*
Backing on to London Fields, this pub has a large decking area, barbecues in the summer and parkside seating where you can watch the sun go down.

## The Mudlark
*London Bridge, SE1 9DA*
The Mudlark has a large outside area with heaters (which is good as the inside is a little small). The garden offers views of Southwark Cathedral and is a great place for a pint after a visit to Borough Market.

## The Crabtree
*Fulham, W6 9HA*
Located right on the river in Fulham, the Crabtree has an enormous garden where you can enjoy the sunshine with a pint. It's a great place to end a walk along the river and there's often a barbecue on the go.

## The Castle
*Islington, N1 9HF*
The roof terrace here has plenty of seating and it's a fantastic place to enjoy a pitcher of Pimm's on a summer's evening.

## The Avalon
*Balham, SW12 9EB*
The Avalon is known for its amazing garden; it has loads of seating and there are heaters and blankets on request if it turns chilly. They do brilliant barbecues but also offer their full menu in the outside areas.

## The Eagle
*Shepherd's Bush, W12 9AZ*
The Eagle has a large walled garden (making it great for kids) with lots of spots in the sun and fairy lights giving a lovely atmosphere. There's a good range of beers and the burgers are worth trying.

## Spaniards Inn
*Hampstead, NW3 7JJ*
A historic pub once frequented by Dick Turpin and John Keats, the Spaniards Inn is full of atmosphere and it's a great place to come for a pint after a walk on Hampstead Heath. The garden is often cited as the best in London and it has loads of space with plenty of tables. A lovely spot to soak up the sun and contemplate the historic surroundings.

## The Dickens Inn
*St Katherine Docks, E1W 1UH*
A big pub situated in one of the old docks. You can imagine the old tall-masted ships coming into the Pool of London, unloading their cargo of ivory. Note the elephants at the entrance to the dock. The beer garden over-looks the harbour and it does the most amazing pizzas ever.

## Vibe Bar
*Brick Lane, E1 6QL*
Located just off Brick Lane, Vibe Bar has a large courtyard area where there's often live music and food on offer.

11

# Do You Know who Once Drank Here?

# Historic Pubs

### Ye Olde Cheshire Cheese
*Fleet Street, EC4A 2BU*
Ye Olde Cheshire Cheese is perhaps one of the most famous historic pubs in London and a tourist destination in its own right. The pub was rebuilt following the Great Fire of London and was a favourite haunt of Samuel Johnson, Tennyson, Dickens, and even Mark Twain and Teddy Roosevelt. It's said that many of Dickens' most famous creations are based on people who visited this dark, character-filled pub. With an ancient vault in its basement, sawdust on the floor and cheap yet delicious Samuel Smith beer on tap, this pub is a 100% must-visit!

### The George Inn
*Southwark, SE1 1NH*
A historic galleried coaching inn where the pilgrims famously gathered before setting off in Chaucer's *Canterbury Tales*. It's worth walking down just to look at the old galleried exterior, even if you don't go in for a drink. Parts of the pub date from 1677 and Dickens wrote about it in *Little Dorrit*.

### The Blackfriar
*Blackfriars, EC4V 4EG*
Located directly outside Blackfriars station, the Blackfriar is a sensational pub for a quiet pint. The pub itself is built on the site of an ancient Dominican priory (hence the name), but the exterior, while impressive enough, fails to do justice to the interior of the establishment, which boasts elaborate carvings, snug seating and other bespoke features. A fantastic location to watch the hectic chaos of City life pass you by (outside) or to enjoy a quiet and civilised pint or meal (inside), this is a can't-miss for anyone looking for a quintessential London pub.

The Blackfriar

### The Tipperary
*Fleet Street, EC4Y 1HT*
A famous pub located across the street from the equally famous Ye Olde Cheshire Cheese. The building itself is older than the Cheese, and the Tipperary's history is just as interesting. An Irish pub through and through, the Tipperary's name comes from the song *It's a Long Way to Tipperary*: it was the last stop for many Irish solders on their way

to France between 1914 and 1918. Its roots as an Irish pub run much deeper, however; this was the first pub outside Ireland to sell Guinness. A must for any fan of history and for fans of a quality pint of the black stuff.

### The Grenadier
*Knightsbridge, SW1X 7NR*
This pub dates from 1763 and in its cobbled courtyard setting looks like an old countryside pub. It is full of Grenadier Guards memorabilia; and the Duke of Wellington was said to have taken his last drink here before the Battle of Waterloo.

### The Olde Bank of England
*Fleet Street, EC4A 2LT*
The pub itself may be new, but the building is steeped in history. Formerly the old Law Courts of the Bank of England, and located next to the High Courts, this impressive building boasts a massive hand-carved oak central bar, ornate ceiling paintings and the sort of pomp and circumstance you would expect from a former Law Court so closely located to the seat of English civil jurisprudence. Well worth a trip for those wishing to experience the living history of British law (when all the lawyers pile in around 5pm) or those interested in

The Olde Bank of England

The Blue Anchor

having a quality London-brewed pint in a stunning architectural setting.

### The Blue Anchor
*Hammersmith, W6 9DJ*
This riverside venue is one of several claiming to be the oldest pub around. The licence details they have date back to 1722! It's a great place to watch rowing boats speed under Hammersmith Bridge and their top-floor dining room has great views out over the river. Outside the pub, there are benches looking out over the water. Good range of ales and good food: an all-round proper pub!

### Lamb and Flag
*Covent Garden, WC2E 9EB*
Good old-fashioned pub with a lovely fireplace. An alleyway behind it makes you forget you're in the middle of touristy Covent Garden.

### Princess Louise
*Holborn, WC1V 7BW*
Allegedly, even the men's toilets in this pub are listed. The pub has a central bar surrounded by a number of enclosed areas that would originally have divided drinkers according to their social class. The details on the mirrors and glass dividers are absolutely stunning.

# Perfect Pints

### De Hems
*Soho, W1D 5BW*
Serving a wide range of ales, from Leffe Blonde and Hoegaarden on tap and a variety of bottled fruit beers, the atmosphere here is cosy, with traditional décor, and they also serve a variety of delicious Dutch snacks.

### The Porterhouse
*Covent Garden, WC2E 7NA*
Suits, students and tourists pack out the front beer terrace every night of the week, while the dark interior lends a more intimate air to enjoy a few ales. A large selection of guest beers, and a number of ales, stouts and lagers from the Porterhouse Brewery make this a refreshing change to the many bland bars in the Covent Garden area.

**Tip**
Waiting for the train or meeting someone at Waterloo station and have some time to kill? Head out of the station's front entrance, look under the railway arches and you'll find the Hole in the Wall pub. A friendly atmosphere, good ale and – rather enjoyably – the building shakes every time a train rumbles over it!

### The Market Porter
*Southwark, SE1 9AA*
In an area that has a lot of choice for the beer connoisseur (The Rake and Brew Wharf, to name just two), this pub always has a stunning range of beers on tap which are always well served.

The Market Porter

### The Harp
*Covent Garden, WC2N 4HS*
Eight ales are always on tap at this pub and its credibility is assured by the fact that it won CAMRA National Pub of the Year in 2011.

### The Bricklayer's Arms
*Putney, SW15 1DD*
This hidden gem is popular with the CAMRA crowd and has won several awards over the years. They have a great range of ales, with many revolving guest varieties, and they also host frequent ale and cider festivals throughout the year. The beer garden is a lovely suntrap and a great place to enjoy a pint on a sunny evening.

**NOT THE KING'S HEAD**

# Strangest Pub Names

- The Hung, Drawn and Quartered, Tower Hill
- Ship and Shovell, Charing Cross
- The Walrus and The Carpenter, Monument
- The Elusive Camel, Victoria
- The Only Running Footman, Mayfair
- Goose and Granite, Fulham
- The Coal Hole, Charing Cross
- The Moon Under Water, Leicester Square

- The Rat and Parrot, South Kensington
- The Bleeding Heart, Farringdon
- Crusting Pipe, Covent Garden
- The Hand and Shears, Smithfield
- The Boot and Flogger, Borough.

*Star-Struck*

# Great Places to Spot Celebs

### The Mulberry Bush
*South Bank, SE1 9PP*
Situated on the South Bank, this pub is a pioneer for the chic gastro experience. Not only does it serve amazing food and a wide range of beers and ales, but as it's located opposite the ITV studios, it's a bit of a celeb hangout, so you never know who might pop in for a drink.

### The Ivy
*Soho, WC2H 9NQ*

The Ivy has a reputation as the ultimate place to spot celebrities. Apart from the chance to see famous fellow-diners, though, the Ivy provides some great food in a glamorous 1920s setting, making it a special night out even if the celebrities decide to stay at home.

### Zuma
*Knightsbridge, SW7 1DL*
A high-end Japanese restaurant, Zuma has been frequented by Beyoncé, Jay-Z and the Beckhams. The open kitchen and sushi bar make for a great atmosphere, but the food is pricey and you will definitely need a reservation!

### The Hawley Arms
*Camden, NW1 8QU*
Made famous by Camden locals like Amy Winehouse and Pete Doherty, the Hawley Arms is known in its own right as a great pub to grab a drink in Camden. There's a brilliant roof terrace where you can enjoy the sunshine while keeping an eye out for famous faces.

COOL AND CLASSY

# Choice Cocktails

### 69 Colebrooke Row
*Islington, N1 8AA*
Located in a quiet street in Islington, you need to keep a sharp eye out to find the small sign which identifies the location of 69 Colebrooke Row. This is a small, understated bar, but what it lacks in size it makes up for in quality. The bartenders are all masters of mixology and the owner, Tony, even has his own cocktail lab upstairs. The cocktails are mixed to focus on the real flavours and because the bar's so popular it's advisable to book a table. You can even reserve a stool at the bar and watch the masters at work or enrol in one of their cocktail classes.

ment of the Breakfast Club and entrance is only permitted by use of a code word. Once permission is granted, a waitress escorts you through the restaurant, stopping only to open a fridge, which you soon realise isn't a fridge at all but really the secret entrance to this uber-cool prohibition-inspired bar. The service is superb and the drinks are pretty good too. Be sure to ask to see 'The Mayor'!

### Be At One
*Clapham, SW4 7AA and other locations*
With great music and fun bartenders a visit to Be At One is always a blast. The great happy hour prices make it even better!

> " The cocktails at Light Bar are the best I've ever had, with something for everyone. "

### The Mayor of Scaredy Cat Town
*Spitalfields, E1 7LS*
An elusive underground cocktail bar, this is definitely a place to visit, even if it's just for the experience. It's set in the base-

The Zetter Townhouse

### The Light Bar
*Leicester Square, WC2N 4HX*
Very pricey cocktails, but that is what they specialise in! There is no name on the door, but you should be able to find it as it's located in the huge foyer of St Martin's Lane Hotel.

### The American Bar at The Savoy
*The Strand, WC2R 0EU*
Recently re-opened after the hotel was refurbished, the bar's interior still has the same old-school glamour. It is London's oldest cocktail bar, complete with jazz pianist and waiters in white gloves. If you have to wait for a table you

can look around the small museum in the bar's lobby (and they will bring you a G&T to keep you going!).

### The Zetter Townhouse

*Farringdon, EC1V 4JJ*

Packed with antique furniture and oddities, this cocktail bar is part of a boutique hotel. Award-winning Tony Conigliaro (of 69 Colebrooke Row fame) is the master mixologist here and the range of cocktails is highly praised. The Bloody Mary is a favourite but the staff are happy to make recommendations if you can't choose.

### Skylon

*South Bank, SE1 8XX*

Part of the South Bank Centre, Skylon is an open space with large windows that allow you to take in stunning views over the Thames. Popular with pre-theatregoers, there is also a restaurant but the cocktail bar is a great place to take visitors or a date so that you can enjoy the view while sipping your drink.

### The Player

*Soho, W1F 8HN*

Very unassuming and hidden-away cocktail bar with a great atmosphere and a huge range of cocktails.

 I highly recommend mixing up the entrées at the Living Room tapas-style. Yum!

### The Living Room

*Soho, W1B 4BE*

Not cheap, but there's a huge selection of great cocktails. Located in a cute little laneway off Piccadilly, the Living Room has a great vibe and lovely food.

### The Experimental Cocktail Club

*Soho, W1D 5PS*

The entrance is a little black door hidden in the middle of Chinatown. It's an odd place, but nevertheless it feels exclusive and therefore makes you feel special! Once you're inside, there are two small levels with barmen shaking away.

### 5th View

*Piccadilly, W1J 9LE*

Located on the top floor of the Waterstones bookstore in Piccadilly, 5th View is a great place to escape after work or a hard day shopping. The bar offers amazing views: try to book a table at the window so that you can enjoy them while sipping your cocktail. Martinis are made at your table and there's also a food menu if you fancy a bite to eat.

### The Star at Night

*Soho, W1F 8FR*

Soho's oldest family-owned bar, the Star at Night has been in the same family for 79 years. A café during the day, the venue turns into a buzzing cocktail bar at night. Go along to a London Gin Club event for tastings and a wide selection of gins.

# London on the Cheap

## Things to Do for Free

**Everyone knows that London can be an expensive place to live, so why not check out our favourite free things to do and save a few pennies!**

### Birdwatching

Walk from Kew Bridge to Richmond along the river to look for herons or keep an eye out in Southwest London for green parakeets squawking overhead. You can also go to the Tate Modern from July to September to look for the pair of peregrine falcons that use this as their nesting site each year. Members of the Royal Society for the Protection of Birds (RSPB) are on hand to help you look through a telescope and tell you a little bit more about the birds.

### Be enchanted by evensong in Westminster Abbey

Evensong takes place in the Abbey at 5pm on Mondays, Tuesdays, Thursdays and Fridays. The singing is enchanting and it's a really special experience. Entry is free and it's a much nicer way to enjoy the Abbey as there are fewer tourists wandering about.

### Visit City Hall

Although people have mixed views of the building, you can visit City Hall free of charge and explore any exhibitions it has on show. London Assembly meetings are open to members of the public if you're interested in the running of the city.

### Cycling along the river

There are a number of great bike routes through the city, but a particular favourite is to start at Hampton Court and cycle to Windsor. It's a beautiful view all the way to Windsor and if you get really tired you can then catch the train back!

### Free museums

A lot of London's museums, including the Science Museum and the Victoria and Albert (V&A), are free to visit, but the Geffrye Museum is a slightly unusual museum that's a real treat. The 11 rooms of the Geffrye Museum depict domestic interiors as they would have looked from 1600 through to the present day.

# Great Residents
# Blue Plaques

It's lovely, and often humbling, to wander around the city keeping an eye out for the blue plaques, learning where some of the city's great minds, influential figures and admired heroes were born, lived and worked.

### Six musicians
- Frédéric Chopin: 4 St James's Place, SW1A 1NP (Left this house to give his last public performance at the Guildhall)
- George Frideric Handel: 25 Brook Street, W1K 4HB (Lived and died here)
- Jimi Hendrix: 23 Brook Street, W1K 4HA (Lived here)
- John Lennon: 34 Montagu Square, W1H 2LJ (Lived here)
- Wolfgang Amadeus Mozart: 180 Ebury Street, SW1W 8UP (Composed his first symphony here)
- Ivor Novello: 11 Aldwych, WC2B 4DG (Lived and died here).

### Five authors
- Arthur Conan Doyle: 12 Tennison Road, SE25 5RT (Lived here)
- Ian Fleming: 22 Ebury Street, SW1W 8LW (Lived here)
- A. A. Milne: 13 Mallord Street, SW3 6DT (Lived here)
- Rudyard Kipling: 43 Villiers Street, WC2N 6NE (Lived here)
- Mary Shelley: 24 Chester Square, SW1W 9HS (Lived here).

### Four inventors
- David Edward Hughes (microphone): 94 Great Portland Street, W1W 7NU (Lived here)
- Samuel Morse (Morse code): 141 Cleveland Street, W1T 6QC (Lived here)
- John Logie Baird (television): 22 Frith Street, W1D 4RP (Demonstrated TV here)
- Alan Turing (computer science pioneer): 2 Warrington Crescent, W9 1ER (Born here).

### Three Prime Ministers (before they moved to Downing Street)
- Richard Clement Attlee: 17 Monkhams Avenue, IG8 0HB (Lived here)
- Neville Chamberlain: 37 Eaton Square, SW1W 9DH (Lived here)
- David Lloyd George: 3 Routh Road, SW18 3SW (Lived here).

### Two medical heroes
- Florence Nightingale: 10 South Street, W1K 1DE (Lived and died here)
- Douglas Macmillan (founder of Macmillan Cancer Support): 15 Ranelagh Road, SW1V 3EX (Lived here).

### And one person you would think was born in London but wasn't
Charles Dickens: 48 Doughty Street, WC1N 2LX (Lived here).

Treat Yourself

# Delightful Afternoon Tea

### Bea's of Bloomsbury

*Bloomsbury, WC1X 8NW and other locations*

Enjoy afternoon tea while you admire the quirky décor of the various locations of Bea's of Bloomsbury. It's famous for its cupcakes, but afternoon tea at Bea's provides savoury baguettes, scones, your choice of tea, treats like brownies and meringues, as well as the cupcake of the day. At the St Paul's location there is the option to have champagne afternoon tea and in the summer months you can have your afternoon tea to take away in a hamper. Booking is advisable, especially for the weekend.

### Mad Hatter's Tea at the Sanderson

*Marylebone, W1T 3NG*

The Mad Hatter's Afternoon Tea isn't your traditional afternoon tea, but if you're

Mad Hatter's Tea at the Sanderson

after something a little different you'll find a culinary adventure with lollipops that taste both hot and cold, multi-coloured sandwiches and Alice-inspired 'Drink me' smoothies and 'Eat me' cakes.

### The National Portrait Gallery

*Leicester Square, WC2H 0HE*

Afternoon tea at the National Portrait Gallery offers scrummy sandwiches, great cakes and amazing value. The staff are very friendly and it's great to visit some of the many amazing famous and historic pieces of artwork after your tea and scones!

### The Berkeley Hotel

*Knightsbridge, SW1X 7RL*

Afternoon tea is prêt-à-porter, with cakes inspired by designers like Alexander McQueen, Anya Hindmarch and Philip Treacy, in the shape of dresses, bags and hats.

### Soho's Secret Tea Rooms

*Soho, W1D 5DH*

Vintage heaven! Soho's Secret Tea Rooms are decked out in 1950s décor, including wonderfully mismatched china. It's located above the Coach and Horses pub: you need to tell the bar staff why you're there and they'll direct you upstairs. The loose leaf teas and fairy cakes are great and make for a good value treat. The perfect escape from busy Soho.

**Tip**
For a great child-friendly afternoon tea try the Stupendous Afternoon Tea at the Mercer Street Hotel. Inspired by Roald Dahl's stories, the tea includes Tremendously Terrific Trifle and Magic Milkshakes.

### The Ritz
*Mayfair, W1J 9BR*
The Ritz is famous for its afternoon tea, with 17 different teas on offer, delicate sandwiches and delicious pastries. Booking in advance is essential; for weekend bookings the hotel advises reserving a slot three to five months in advance.

### The Orangery
*Kensington Palace, W8 4PX*

Set in Queen Anne's 18th-century conservatory in Kensington Palace Gardens, the Orangery's historic surroundings provide the perfect backdrop for tea, scones and sandwiches, and you can sit outside on the terrace taking in the views of the gardens. The Orangery doesn't take bookings, so try to go early to avoid queuing.

### Teanamu Chaya Teahouse
*Notting Hill, W11 1DP*
Tea artisan Pei Wang has created a haven for tea lovers – the tranquil setting, amazing scones with rose petal jam and incredible selection of teas make this a wonderful experience. Don't expect a standard three-tier cake stand type of afternoon tea, but you will learn how to perform a Chinese tea ceremony. Only open at weekends.

### Athenaeum Hotel
*Mayfair, W1J 7BJ*
Winner of the 2012 Top London Tea Award from the Tea Guild, the Athenaeum offers a wonderful afternoon tea experience in the lovely setting of their Garden Room. They have friendly, knowledgeable staff and offer a honey tea which features a menu made up of items containing local Regent's Park honey.

### Dean Street Townhouse
*Soho, W1D 3SE*
This is the place to go for brilliant value for money. With its comfy armchairs in a relaxed and cosy atmosphere, Dean Street Townhouse offers delicious scones and is a great place to go if you've been wandering around Oxford Street.

**Tip**
If you're looking for a more manly version of a traditional afternoon tea, try Sanctum's Gentleman's Afternoon Tea. The steak sandwiches, cigars and selection of Jack Daniels transform the ritual of afternoon tea into a more macho experience.

# Veggie Restaurants

# (That Aren't Pizza Places or Curry Houses)

**The London vegetarian is more spoiled for choice than ever. From a Michelin recommendation to cheap and cheerful cafés, here are some of our favourites.**

### Vanilla Black

*Chancery Lane, EC4A 1LB*
A Michelin recommended restaurant, this is the place to go for gourmet vegetarian cuisine. With imaginative dishes, such as fried mushroom mousse and tarragon waffles, and exquisite service, this is a delightful place for a special night out.

Vanilla Black

### The Gate

*Hammersmith, W6 9QL and Islington EC 1V 4NN*
Reasonably priced gourmet veggie cuisine in an attractive room in an old church hall. Occasionally there's a pianist playing, and in the summer you can eat at the handful of tables in the outdoor courtyard.

### Mildreds

*Soho, W1F 9AN*
Established in 1988, Mildreds offers friendly service in a lively atmosphere. It's excellent value for money for a central London location, with an eclectic mix of vegetarian and vegan dishes, many of which are gluten- and wheat-free. From stews and curries to Asian cuisine and salads, the menu offers a range of dishes from across the globe. The pudding list is also divine and most of the desserts are suitable for vegans.

Green Note

## Green Note

*Camden, NW1 7AN*
Green Note offers loads of imaginative vegetarian tapas dishes at very affordable prices, and great live music in a very intimate and friendly environment.

## Manna

*Primrose Hill, NW3 3AJ*
London's oldest veggie restaurant (44 years and counting), run by a Californian couple who do a pumpkin-based Thanksgiving dinner every November.

Thali dish at Manna

## The Riverside Vegetaria

*Kingston-upon-Thames, KT1 1HN*
Located in a quirky green building on Kingston High Street, this cosmopolitan restaurant sits on the banks of the Thames and offers an eclectic menu.

## Tibits

*Piccadilly Circus, W1B 4DA*
Tibits provides a healthy veggie buffet with around 40 hot and cold options available at any time. You pay by the

Tibits

weight and then get a free bread roll. The juice blends are yummy too, and the large upstairs dining area has a funky yet relaxed vibe with flock wallpaper and fine tunes. Downstairs there's an area for kids, so everyone can enjoy a meal here.

## Saf

*Kensington, W8 5SE*
Entirely vegan, mostly raw, the menu at Saf is always fascinating and there's a great list of alcoholic and non-alcoholic cocktails.

## Blah, Blah, Blah

*Twickenham, TW1*
Formerly based in Shepherd's Bush, this restaurant is excellent value with inventive food, BYO booze and crayons are provided so you can doodle on the paper tablecloths!

## Food for Thought

*Covent Garden, WC2H 9PR*
A Covent Garden landmark, Food for Thought is a basement café that's always busy. BYO bottle.

" Tibits is a veggie/vegan haven. "

# Wonderful World Cuisine

**London is known as a multicultural mixing pot, so why not be a bit adventurous and try one of the more exotic cuisines which are on offer in the city?**

### Kimchee: Korean

*Holborn, WC1V 6EA*
The best Korean restaurant in London that gives you a taste of Seoul – the raw beef yuk hwae are incredible.

### Yalla Yalla: Lebanese

*Fitzrovia, W1W 8HQ and other locations*
Offers the most amazing Lebanese street food. The hummus shawarma with flatbread is the best thing on the menu.

### Au Lac: Vietnamese

*Highbury Park, N5 2XE*
The best takeaway Vietnamese dinner: their chicken noodle soup makes you feel better instantly.

### Tas/EV: Turkish

*Farringdon, EC1M 3JB and other locations*
There are a few of these around London (EV is another version of the Tas restaurants) and they all serve a huge selection of brilliant Turkish food. Great for lunch or dinner, they also do good set menus if you are looking for a bargain. The lamb dishes are particularly good, and they also offer an excellent vegetarian selection.

### Mandalay: Burmese

*Paddington, W2 1EG*
This restaurant is such a unique experience, and it is very cheap. It's also really hard to find Burmese food in London, so be sure to check this out!

*Spuntino in Soho does the best Negronis.*

Dolsot bibimbap at Kimchee

### Simurgh: Persian

*Covent Garden, WC2E 9BL*
Great food and lovely staff who'll adapt meals if you need it. They also put on belly dancing on Fridays and Saturdays if you want some entertainment with your meal!

### Mosob: Eritrean

*Westbourne Park, W9 3RB*
Serving delicious East African food, Mosob is a family business with friendly and charming staff who are eager to teach visitors about their country. The restaurant also has a spectacular coffee ceremony.

# Sensational Slices
# Great Pizza Places

### Santa Maria
*Ealing, W5 5RA*
Offering the most authentic Neapolitan pizza in West London, Santa Maria is small – so you'll probably need to wait for a table. The wood-fired oven creates great pizza, though, so it's worth the wait and it's really good value for money.

Tip

Try Franco Manca in Chiswick for huge and delicious freshly made pizzas from a stone oven.

### Flatplanet
*Soho, W1F 7JG*
A different take on pizza. Flatplanet serves up flatbreads with a range of toppings. For a quick lunch with lots of garlic sauce, the El Diablo is a favourite, made on a spelt bread with chorizo, harissa, rocket, sundried tomato and hot sauce.

### Pizza Metro
*Battersea Rise, SW11 1EQ*
This is a small, authentic Italian restaurant where the staff are brilliant and the selection of pizzas is huge. If your group wants to order a few different toppings, they merge your order together – the toppings are still separate but you end up with one giant pizza! This way of serving is really good for sharing as you end up trying things you would normally never have ordered. They also have a restaurant in Notting Hill.

### Pizza East
*Shoreditch, E1 6JJ and Westbourne Park, W10 5TA*
The Shoreditch location is in a former warehouse and the other restaurant is in an old pub. The trendy interiors at Pizza East are the ultimate in toned-down chic. There's a great atmosphere at the shared tables and the wood-fired ovens and open-plan kitchens serve up brilliant pizzas with great bases and quirky toppings like potato and veal meatballs.

Margherita pizza at Pizza East

# A Taste of the Country

# Top Farmers' Markets

### Pimlico Farmers' Market

*Orange Square, corner of Pimlico Road and Ebury Street, SW1W 8UT*

Every Saturday, from 9am to 1pm, at what locals call the 'Orange Square', is one of the prettiest farmers' markets in London. A stone's throw from the bustle of the King's Road, this almost rustic market offers everything from a dedicated tomato stall to duck, venison and buffalo meat!

### Maltby Street Market

*Bermondsey, SE1*

The alternative, less touristy version of Borough Market. Set under old railway arches, Maltby Street Market is open on Saturdays from 9am to 2pm. You'll find a great selection of bakers, independent breweries and a fabulous choice of cheeses with Dutch and Swiss specialities on offer.

### Oval Farmers' Market

*St Mark's Church, Kennington, SE11 4PW*

With a wonderful range of food and drink, this market is perfect for picking up weekend lunch or picnics, as well as filling the fridge for the week ahead. Fruit and veg, breads and baked things, amazing pies, juices, meat, fish, and sausage sandwiches for munching while you wander around. The market runs on Saturdays from 10am to 3pm.

### Marylebone Farmers' Market

*Cramer Street Car Park, Marylebone, W1U 4EW*

A market with a genuine neighbourhood feel, Marylebone offers high-quality fish, meat and produce, and it isn't too big or overwhelming. The market is open on Sundays from 10am to 2pm.

Fruit juice stall at Marylebone Farmers' Market

### Queen Mary Farmers' Market

*Queen Mary Campus, Mile End Road, E1 4NS*

It's out in the East End and a little different from your average affair, providing great fresh produce to the student population. The market is open on Thursdays from 9am to 2pm and sells meat, cheese, fish and great local fruit and veg.

# Tasty
# Thai

## Siam Central

*Fitzrovia, W1T 2LX*

Perfect for getting a decent meal quickly and inexpensively. The curries are full of flavour and the drunken noodles are highly praised.

## The Pepper Tree

*Clapham Common, SW4 7AB*

The most authentic-tasting Thai food in London and really affordable too. The pad thai noodles with prawns are incredible and the atmosphere is great as you share long tables with other diners. Be warned – there's often a queue!

## Yvonne's Thai Cuisine

*In the King's Arms pub, Waterloo, SE1 8TB*

Hidden at the back of a traditional pub, Yvonne's does inexpensive, wonderfully tasty curry and pad thai dishes. You order your food at your table and go up to get drinks from the bar, which makes for a bustling atmosphere with delicious food.

## Busaba Eathai

*Tottenham Court Road, W1F 0TR and other locations*

Really delicious Thai food with quick service and open-plan tables that you share with fellow diners. This really adds to the atmosphere of the place. If there is a queue it usually moves quickly. The ginger tea and biscuits are brilliant and the food is really affordable.

## Talad Thai

*Putney, SW15 6TL*

The décor might seem a little basic, but the Thalad Thai does one of the best red curries ever. The starters are fantastic and this is the perfect place if you're in the mood for inexpensive, tasty Thai fare.

## The Churchill Arms

*Kensington, W8 7LN*

Expectations shouldn't be too high when you first walk into this pub; it's very old-fashioned with a dark wood bar. However, at the back of the pub is a restaurant that resembles a greenhouse – its ceiling and walls are covered in plants and flowers – which serves the most amazing Thai food. Not only is the food delicious but the price is right, too; dishes are no more than about £8 each. If you prefer you can stay in the pub area to eat, sitting around the real open fire. Be wary that it tends to get busy after work, but definitely give it a go and make sure to try the pad thai.

Yvonne's Thai at the King's Arms

# Restaurants with Stunning Views

**London boasts some incredible views and enjoying them whilst having a meal can be a really special night out, whether for a spectacular first date or to celebrate a special event. Here's our pick of the restaurants with the best views.**

### Madison

*St Paul's, EC4M 9AF*
Madison boasts an open-air terrace with views of the iconic St Paul's Cathedral. The restaurant offers breakfast, lunch and dinner, or you can enjoy a drink from the extensive wine list as you soak up the view.

### Portrait

*National Portrait Gallery, Leicester Square, WC2H 0HE*
The restaurant at the top of the National Portrait Gallery is a hidden gem, with views over Trafalgar Square, Big Ben and the London Eye. It is quite pricey, but the food is delicious. Get there before it gets dark and watch the lights come on over London as the light fades. When you're stuffed full and don't feel like walking anywhere else, you can spend some time wandering around the gallery beneath.

**Tip**
If you just want a drink while enjoying views of the city, try the Boundary Rooftop, the Tate 7th Floor or the Brera Bar at the Lyric Hammersmith.

Portrait at the National Portrait Gallery

### Browns

*London Bridge, SE1 2YG*
One of the nicest versions of this chain. It's great in the summer when you can sit outside and admire the views of the River Thames and Tower Bridge — always impressive! They also provide an excellent selection of cocktails at reasonable prices. Make sure to try the sharing platters, in particular the fish one.

View from Inn the Park

## Galvin at Windows Restaurant and Bar

*Park Lane Hilton Hotel, Mayfair, W1K 1BE*
You can enjoy some fantastic French cuisine at this Michelin-starred restaurant while admiring the stunning 360-degree views from your vantage point on the 28th floor of the famous Park Lane Hilton Hotel.

## Babylon at Kensington Roof Gardens

*Kensington, W8 5SA*
An oasis in the middle of Kensington: you won't believe you're still in the city. Discover different garden themes, such as Spanish and traditional English, as you wander the various paths of the 1.5 acres of roof gardens. There are even some resident flamingos! The menu is incredible, too, making this a really special place to enjoy a meal.

## Restaurant at the Petersham Hotel

*The Petersham Hotel, Richmond, TW10 6UZ*
Located on the top of Richmond Hill, the restaurant in the Petersham Hotel offers stunning panoramic views over the Thames and the surrounding green areas, coupled with impressive service

and a delightful menu. Make sure you book in advance to secure a window seat.

## The Paramount

*Top of Centre Point, Tottenham Court Road, WC1A 1DD*
Great restaurant with a viewing bar around the edge to give you a 360-degree view of the capital. The lounge is west facing, so it's a wonderful place to enjoy a cocktail at sunset.

## Inn the Park

*St James's Park, SW1A 2BJ*
Found in the middle of St James's Park, Inn the Park has great views of its natural surroundings. It's a modern café with an outdoor seating area. It can be busy with tourists but it's normally quieter for dinner.

## OXO

*South Bank, SE1 9PH*
Situated on the eighth floor of the Oxo Tower, this is the place to take visitors or for a special occasion. Try to book a table at the window so that you can take in the views of the Thames and St Paul's. Make sure you have a drink on the balcony before your meal so you can really appreciate the view.

Oxo Tower Bar

# Recommended Revelry

# Fantastic Festivals and Events

**Throughout the year you'll always be able to find a great festival or an event like a carnival or a food fair somewhere in the city. Here's our list of just a few of the great events that take place in London.**

### ■ Taste of London
*Regent's Park*
The Taste of London fair is held in June and it's real foodie heaven. There are hundreds of stalls with delicious samples, and demonstrations from high-end restaurants and celebrity chefs to inspire those tastebuds. There are also wine stalls and tasting plates from over 40 of London's top restaurants. The Christmas Taste of London fair is a seperate event held in December that really gets you in the festive spirit!

### ■ The Proms
*Royal Albert Hall, SW7 2AP*
The BBC Proms is a great chance to expand your musical taste and experience classical music in  the august setting of the Royal Albert Hall. The concerts run for eight weeks starting in July and there are also some special Proms in the Park concerts. Even if you're not normally a fan of classical music, the atmosphere at the concerts is infectious and there are special themes for some concerts, such as movie soundtracks (including spaghetti westerns), *Doctor Who* and special performances by stars like Jamie Cullum.

### ■ Country Living Christmas Fair
*Business Design Centre, Islington, N1 0QH*
A mammoth fair with hundreds of exhibitors that gives you the chance to get extra special and original presents, decorations, food and treats for yourself! The fair is organised by *Country Living* magazine and normally takes places in November.

### ■ BFI Film Festival
*BFI South Bank and various other venues*
Taking place in October each year, the BFI London Film Festival is the UK's largest film event and gives movie fans the chance to attend screenings of over 300 features, including shorts, documentaries and beloved classics such as *Chinatown* and *Breakfast at Tiffany's*. The programme also includes Q&A sessions and educational events.

## Notting Hill Carnival

*Notting Hill*

The Notting Hill Carnival is one of the biggest street festivals, celebrating London's diversity with Caribbean music, dance and costume, and finishing off with a famous mass band parade. The carnival is usually held during the late August bank holiday and, while it's very busy, it's a vibrant and exciting day out.

## Open House London

*Various locations*

The Open House weekend is a free event held in September which gives Londoners the chance to explore some of the city's best architecture and learn more about the stunning buildings that make up the capital's character. From the Bank of England to the BBC Television Centre, the tours give you a unique chance to uncover some of the secrets of these iconic buildings.

## Hampton Court Flower Show

*Hampton Court*

Each July sees Hampton Court play host to the largest flower show in the world, giving visitors the chance to enjoy stunning garden displays in the beautiful setting of Henry VIII's Tudor palace.

Visitors have the opportunity to buy plants and accessories, and there is an emphasis on environmental issues, such as teaching visitors to grow their own vegetables.

## Mayor's Thames Festival

*From Westminster Bridge to Tower Bridge*

The Mayor's Thames Festival is a free event that takes place in September each year. The event includes art, music, food, dancing and river racing, all culminating in a Night Carnival with a lavish fireworks display over the river. It's a brilliant way to celebrate the end of summer without spending a penny.

## Pearly King Harvest Festival

*From Guildhall Yard to St Mary-le-Bow church*

This is the best place to see the pearly kings and queens in all their glory as they lead a parade from the Guildhall Yard to St Mary-le-Bow church for a harvest festival service in October. All proceeds from the service are donated to charity and seeing all the 'pearlies' in their 'smother' suits is a true London experience.

> ❝ Go to the Summer Exhibition at the Royal Academy or the Proms — big events are what London is all about. ❞

# Top Wine Lists and Merchants

### RSJ Restaurant

*Waterloo, SE1 9NR*
Great neighbourhood restaurant in a converted 19th-century stable with an extensive wine list dominated by wines from the Loire.

### Le Cassoulet

*Croydon, CR2 6PA*
Award-winning French restaurant with interesting and good value French wines. The wine list has some really helpful descriptions.

### 28–50 Wine Workshop and Kitchen

*Fleet Street, EC4A 1BT*
A French bistro and wine bar, 28–50 offers the option to try wines by the glass, the carafe or the bottle, giving you ample opportunity to try something from their well-chosen list. In case you're wondering about the name, 28–50 refers to the degrees of latitude between which most of the world's wines are grown.

### Chez Bruce

*Wandsworth Common, SW17 7EG*
Often praised for its food (and deservedly so), Chez Bruce is also renowned for its wine list. The diverse and interesting list appeals to both fine wine lovers and non-experts, and it's obvious why Chez Bruce has won awards for its wine list. The list offers great quality for reasonable prices.

### Berry Bros. & Rudd

*Green Park, SW1A 1EG*
With one of the best shop fronts in London, Berry Bros. & Rudd, established in 1698, has one of the best selections of wines in the city.

### Philglas and Swiggot

*Marylebone, W1H 7SB, Battersea, SW11 1NG and Richmond, TW10 6UB*
A great selection, knowledgeable staff and a relaxed atmosphere. There's also a great choice of glasses and glassware if you're looking for a gift.

### Wine Pantry

*Borough Market, SE1 9AA*
Only stocks English fine wines, cheese and meats, making this an absolute gem for sitting outside on sunny afternoons and soaking up the atmosphere of the market.

**Tip**
The oldest wine bar in London, Gordon's Wine Bar features a diverse wine list, which customers can enjoy by candlelight while seated in historic caverns. Gordon's is *always* busy so you'll need to be there early (before the after-work crowd) to get a seat.

# A Little Je Ne Sais Quoi

# Fantastic French Fare

### L'Art du Fromage

*Chelsea, SW10 0JL*

A really unusual French restaurant in London terms. Two French friends opened it together and it is all about cheese! The raclette and fondue are 'all you can eat' and are so good!

### Le Mercury

*Islington, N1 1QY*

This place has a cosy, cute and romantic atmosphere with candles in wine bottles on tables and chequered tablecloths. The food is tasty and great value – you can get three courses for two people with a bottle of wine for about £40!

### Le Garrick

*Covent Garden, WC2E 9BH*

A small treasure located in Covent Garden, Le Garrick offers classic French dishes in a great atmosphere. Fantastic for a pre-theatre meal or a romantic evening.

### Le Petit Auberge

*Islington, N1 2TZ*

A great quality French bistro, with good prices and friendly staff, and – most important of all – delicious food!

### Morgan M

*Barbican, EC1A 9EJ*

The seared fillet of sea bass on carrot and ginger risotto is incredible. Deserts are also a good reason to go; make sure you try the vanilla rice pudding with an orange tuille and pina colada sorbet.

### Mon Plaisir

*Covent Garden, WC2H 9DD*

An excellent old-fashioned French bistro. The restaurant serves excellent but unpretentious French food, and it has a lovely, cosy atmosphere.

### The French Café

*Tooting Bec, SW17 8QD*

Tucked down a residential street in south London, the French Café is a bit off the beaten track, but it's a real gem. The food is very authentically French with a good selection of starters, mains and really delicious desserts. They do a *prix fixe* menu where you can get a starter and a main course for only £10, and the options on this menu are always good. They also have outdoor seating surrounded by lavender bushes.

Le Garrick

# Sweet
# Treats

### Prestat
*Piccadilly, SW1Y 6DS*
Step into this tiny shop in the elegant Princes Arcade and breathe in! The chocolates are so good that they have a Royal Warrant from the Queen.

### Choccywoccydoodah
*Soho, W1F 7PS*
Entering this shop is like stepping into Willy Wonka's factory. Famous for its spectacular wedding cakes, the shop is full of handmade creations like chocolate animals, truffles, lollipops and dipped marshmallows. There's also a café upstairs serving hot chocolate, cakes, ice cream sundaes and all manner of goodies.

Choccywoccydoodah

### Nardulli
*Clapham Common, SW4 0JE*
Beautiful, authentic Italian ice cream and sorbets with a large range of delicious favours – from the familiar (vanilla or amaretto) to the more experimental (cardamom or liquorice). Perfect for a hot summer's day, but it's open pretty much all year round. You can even order a tub to have at home!

### Gino Gelato
*Charing Cross, WC2N 4HZ*
Pretty much any flavour of ice cream you could imagine – the tiramisu is a particular highlight. If you're feeling brave, try the Chianti and chocolate.

Liquid nitrogen ice cream at the Chin Chin Laboratorists

### Chin Chin Laboratorists
*Camden, NW1 8AF*
The only liquid nitrogen ice cream parlour in Europe, this is definitely the coolest place for ice cream! Your ice cream is made in front of you so you get to see the whole process as the liquid nitrogen is added to the mixer.

# Where to Get a Proper Fry-Up

Top Greasy Spoons

### Tony's Café
*Clapham Junction, SW11 6QL*
Tony's Café has all the essential ingredients: the squeezy ketchup bottles shaped like tomatoes, retro seating – and it always smells of bacon! Tony will recommend the 'smaller' breakfast for the ladies (still massive) and a plate that takes up half the table for the men. It's greasy but yum!

### The Shepherdess
*Shoreditch, EC1V 1JN*
A traditional English café both in décor and menu, the Shepherdess is everything you'd expect: no-frills, traditional food done really well. Egg and chips, bacon sandwiches and tea are all classics and the fact that the café is always busy attests to its quality.

### The River Café
*Putney, SW6 3UH*
A fantastic little greasy spoon which does a mean sausage baguette. All your favourites plus a selection of home-cooked Italian family fare.

### Regency Café
*Westminster, SW1P 4BY*
Most people say this is their epitome of a greasy spoon. The Formica tables, cabbies drinking tea and orders being shouted across to the kitchen all add to the atmosphere. The traditional English breakfast is incredible, the portions are huge and the prices are very reasonable.

### E Pellicci
*Bethnal Green, E2 0AG*
E Pellicci is an Italian café, but it's a mecca for a traditional fry-up. This is a no-frills, family-run café with a brilliant atmosphere at shared tables. The menu is a brilliant mix of English and Italian classics.

Breakfast at Regency Café

### Norwood Cafe
*Croydon, SE25 6EA*
Huge portions for low prices, with friendly staff. You can even substitute items to create your perfect fry-up.

# Classic
# Curry Houses

### Cafe Nawaz
*London Bridge, SE1 3SS*
Located behind Guy's Hospital, Cafe Nawaz offers BYO booze as well as brilliant food. The doctors and nurses from the hospital eat there and listening to their conversations while you enjoy your curry can be quite entertaining!

### Dishoom
*Covent Garden, WC2H 9FB*
The original Bombay café, Dishoom serves incredibly authentic Indian street food in interiors styled on Leopold's – the famed café in Mumbai.

### The Cinnamon Club
*Westminster, SW1P 3BU*
A favourite with politicians, The Cinnamon Club is a very upmarket restaurant that serves modern Indian cuisine in the former Grade II listed Old Westminster Library.

The Cinnamon Club

### Lahore 2
*Commercial Road, E1 2PS*
This place isn't known for its décor (which is café-style), but it's the place to go for authentic food. They offer BYO beer and traditional dishes; there can be queues, but it's worth the wait.

### Tip
If you're looking for a great vegetarian curry restaurant, check out Woodlands, particularly the Marylebone Lane branch. They serve a wide variety of southern Indian dishes.

### The Coriander
*Blackheath, SE3 7EQ and Vauxhall SE11 5HY*
With its relaxed atmosphere and delicious food, The Coriander is reliably good.

### Rara
*Kew, TW9 3LU*
If you love a good curry, this is the place for you. Gorgeous Nepalese dishes with lovely sauces: the butter chicken is delicious. They also do takeaway.

### Trishna
*Marylebone, W1U 3DG*
This is Indian food at its finest. The menu is fresh and different, and the coconut sorbet is to die for! The interior

features exposed brick and there is original artwork hanging on the wall. Well worth going for top-quality food and a fantastic dining experience. It offers an array of seafood dishes and the best lamb chops in London!

### Khan's

*Brixton, SW2 1PE*

Khan's is a real find. Good value for money, authentic dishes and they offer BYO bottle. The portions are huge as well!

### Simply Indian

*Borough, SE1 4LA*

Simply Indian offers fantastic food, cheap drink and a great intimate atmosphere – what more could you want?

### Mirch Masala

*Tooting, SW17 7TG*

This is a little secret gem in Tooting. The curries are probably spicier than you might be used to, but they are all delicious, especially the sizzling lamb tandooris. On Saturday nights there is always a queue of people trying to get a table, so it's advisable to book. They do not serve alcohol, but you are welcome to take your own with you.

> **Tip**
> Brick Lane is often praised as the best place to go for a curry in London – head along to their annual curry festival in May for a great chance to sample different dishes from local restaurants.

# Sushi Shrines

### Sushinho

*Chelsea, SW3 5UH*

Wonderful freshly made sushi with unusual ingredients. The sea urchin on the buri-yellowtail tartare is phenomenal, as is the signature sushinho roll.

### Kulu Kulu

*Soho, W1F 9TU*

If you want a conveyor belt sushi experience but don't want to pay through the nose, Kulu Kulu offers an affordable range of well-prepared sushi dishes. The staff are helpful for first timers as well.

### Café Japan

*Golders Green, NW11 7RR*

Café Japan offers authentic, top-quality sushi at a great price – the butter fish maki is an absolute highlight and the bento boxes are delicious. You can choose to sit at the sushi bar and graze or sit at a table and enjoy the Japanese delights. It's always busy but well worth it if you have to wait.

> **Tip**
> Wasabi has branches across London and is great value for money: their tubs are really big and cost less than £5!

# Delightful
# Delis

## Deli Boutique

*Clapham Junction, SW11 1TQ*
Stepping inside is like stepping into a deli in France. The cheery atmosphere is filled with the smell of homemade crêpes and crème brulées, which are absolutely divine! You can buy a bottle of organic wine and come back to refill your bottle very cheaply straight from the barrel. There is a lovely little garden outside where they will bring you the *plat du jour*. And they bake the baguettes fresh daily!

## Gusto and Relish

*Barnes, SW13 0PZ*
This tasty little delicatessen keeps a low profile in a fairly suburban area of Barnes. It boasts a great selection of olives, patés, cheeses and cured meats, and on Sunday mornings the smell of freshly baked croissants fills the shop. As well as the basics, Gusto and Relish offers a seasonal range of game, veg and berries that are hard to buy elsewhere in London, and some really special finds on its many shelves make it a real foodie's deli.

### Tip
If cheese is your thing, make sure you go to Rippon Cheese Stores in Pimlico. The whole store is a walk-in larder with hundreds of cheeses arranged alphabetically.

## Ottolenghi

*Islington, N1 2TZ and other locations*
This amazing deli, started by the chef Yotam Ottolenghi, is quite pricey but worth it. They do breakfast, pastries, cakes and lunch, with a wide selection of meats, fish, vegetarian dishes and sides. They always have new and interesting combinations going above and beyond your standard deli selection.

Ottolenghi

## North Street Deli

*Clapham, SW4 0HB*
Tucked away from the High Street, this friendly little deli is perfect for lunch and afternoon snacks. They offer a fantastic selection of really well-priced fresh, beautiful homemade food from quiches to salads to sandwiches.

### Menoo

*Kensington, W8 4LL*
An affordable deli in the Kensington area. As well as serving Italian deli-style fresh food on their daily menu (sandwiches, hot and cold dishes – and an amazing selection), they also sell lots of Italian larder products – antipasti, cheeses, biscuits and lots more.

### Fernando's

*Charing Cross, WC2N 4EA*
The quality is a cut above the competition in an area with a lot of similar delis. The owner is a charming bloke from Madeira who always remembers his customers.

## INDULGE YOUR INNER CARNIVORE

# Brilliant Burgers

### Meat Liquor

*Bond Street, W1G 0BA*
For the dirtiest (in a good way), delicious burgers and an electric atmosphere, be sure to get there early to avoid the queues that snake around the block. The burgers are incredible: the Dead Hippie is the one to try.

### Haché

*Camden, NW1 7HJ and other locations*
A great selection of burgers with several topping combinations on the menu (including the Louisiana burger with peanut butter!). There's also a good range of sides like sweet potato chips and nachos.

### Byron

*Hoxton, N1 6PB and other locations*

With quality Scottish beef and a variety of toppings (including several types of cheese), Byron gets it right every time. They also serve great beers (including local London brew Camden Town) and deliciously thick milkshakes. The courgette fries are to die for!

> **Tip**
> For traditional American-style food (ribs, macaroni cheese, pulled pork, etc.), try Bodean's, with locations in Fulham, Clapham, Soho and Tower Hill. The menu is good value for money and while meat is their speciality, they also cater well for vegetarians.

### The Draft House

*Clapham, SW11 6QW and other locations*
Really nice for a Friday night dinner and drinks after work. The staff are really friendly and attentive, and the food is excellent. Be warned: the burgers are epic!

# Finest Fish and Chips

### Rock and Sole Plaice
*Covent Garden, WC2H 9AJ*
A proper chippy – not the microwave variety for

tourists – and you can even sit down outside or down-stairs. Great if you get hungry while wandering around Covent Garden.

### Kennedy's of Goswell Road
*Clerkenwell, EC1V 7DT*
A favourite with cabbies, Kennedy's offers fish and chips to eat in or take away but they also do fantastic pies. The mushy peas are great too. Expensive, but one of the best in London.

### Golden Hind
*Marylebone, W1U 2PN*
With celebrity pictures on the wall, a closely guarded secret batter recipe and lovely chips, this is a real London favourite. The restaurant has a great atmosphere and they offer BYO bottle.

### Fish & Chips
*Soho, W1F 0PY*
Fish & Chips (yes, it's really called that) is a brilliant chippy – it's dirt cheap, serves up huge portions and does a great veggie breakfast.

### The FishClub
*St John's Hill, SW11 1TH and Clapham High Street, SW4 7TG*
You could choose a classic coley and chips, but the FishClub has a really varied menu with oysters, prawn and chorizo kebabs, sweet potato chips, tuna steaks, rocket salads and pots of homemade aioli.

### J. Sheekey
*Leicester Square, WC2N 4AL*
J. Sheekey is a great seafood restaurant that does wonderful fish and chips. The restaurant dates back to 1896 and is situated right in the middle of the theatre district, so it's great for pre- and post-theatre meals. It is very popular with actors and pictures of its famous clients adorn the walls.

### Poppies Fish and Chips
*Spitalfields, E1 6QR*
Fresh fish from Billingsgate market, batter made from a family recipe and lovely thick chips, all wrapped up in mock newspaper. If you decide to sit in you can enjoy the 1950s diner-style restaurant. Make sure you try the mushy peas.

### Fish!
*Borough Market, SE1 9AL and other locations*
Extraordinarily good, fresh fish and chips. It's done traditionally but also appeals to gourmet tastes, with classics like cod through to swordfish. They also do a great range of sides and the restaurant at Borough Market has a lovely outdoor area where you can sit and enjoy your meal.

### Masters Super Fish
*Waterloo Road, SE1 8UX*
The fish is delivered fresh each day and the portions are massive! You can sit in or take away, but sit-in customers get free shrimps and bread and butter while they wait.

*Just Like Mum Used to Make*

# Recommended Roasts

### The Princess of Shoreditch

*Shoreditch, EC2A 4NE*

Away from the hustle and bustle of Old Street, the Princess of Shoreditch is a traditional pub which offers fantastic Sunday roasts. Try to book in advance to be sure of getting a table. It can be pricey, but the lamb, pork belly and generous portions of veg are great. Those with children should be warned that the upstairs restaurant is reached by a slightly scary spiral staircase.

### The Temperance

*Fulham, SW6 3LF*

The perfect place to come and veg out on a Sunday; amazing roasts (choose from chicken, beef and lamb) as well as a tasty nut roast. You can sit for hours and digest the massive portions while admiring the unusual architecture of this former temperance billiard hall.

The Princess of Shoreditch

There's normally a good range of guest ales on tap as well.

**Tip**

The Bowler in Wandsworth Common serves up the most tender pork belly as well as a range of other beautifully presented dishes at great prices.

### Simpson's-in-the-Strand

*The Strand, WC2R 0EW*

A real institution, this is the perfect place for an old-fashioned Sunday roast. The restaurant may haul in the wealthy tourists, but there's a reason – it's a great experience when the waiter rolls the silver domed trolley to the table and carves the meat in front of you.

### Balham Bowls Club

*Balham, SW12 8QX*

This kitsch-style eatery is located close to Balham station and it's a great pub for a lazy Sunday enjoying a roast. There's a beer garden to chill out in and they also do sausage rolls at the bar, which are a big favourite.

# Shopping

Whether you need a gift for a friend's birthday, you're on the hunt for a favourite record or a unique retro garment, or maybe you just want to engage in some retail therapy while browsing one of London's great markets, read on to find the best places to shop until you drop.

# Gorgeous
# Gift Shops

### ■ Aria
*Islington, N1 1PN*
An independent shop selling homewares and gifts with a focus on design, Aria sell a great range including jewellery, kitchen goods, lighting and furniture and stock well-known names (like Orla Kiely and Alessi) as well as up-and-coming designers.

### ■ Huttons
*Kingston, KT1 1TR and other locations*
Huttons is great if you're searching for a special present. They have lovely jewellery, beautiful baby gifts and delightful knick-knacks.

### ■ The Inside Man
*Wandsworth, SW17 7EF*
Finally, a place to go when you need a gift for the man in your life! Whether

you're buying for a boyfriend, father, brother, friend, etc., the range of items on offer (from cufflinks to posters and remote-controlled toys) means you'll always come away with the ideal gift.

### ■ Oliver Bonas
*Hampstead, NW3 1PR and other locations*
Selling a huge range of items from clothes, jewellery and books to home furnishings and baby gifts, as well as gorgeous cards  and wrapping paper, Oliver Bonas is a one-stop shop for present buying.

# It's All Fun and Games
## Top Toyshops

### Sylvanian Families
*Highbury, N5 2LT*
This is a very specialist shop offering the widest range of Sylvanian Families products in Europe. The shop sells the adorably dressed animals and their accessories seven days a week and it's a gorgeous shop crammed with all the collectors' items you could ever need.

### Hamleys
*Regent Street, W1B 5BT*
Hamleys is one of the largest toyshops in the world, and a visit here brings out the inner child in anyone. With over seven floors and all types of toys – from gadgets to soft toys and board games – Hamleys has something for everyone.

### Honeyjam
*Ladbroke Grove, W11 1NN*
A traditional toyshop selling classics like spinning tops and wooden toys for a range of ages. Honeyjam also sells costumes and has a pocket money range that kids will love.

### Pollock's Toy Museum
*Tottenham Court Road, W1T 2HL*
Pollock's is a great place to take children as it's both a museum and a toyshop. Kids will love wandering through it looking at toys from bygone eras, examining china dolls and Victorian teddy bears. Kids also relish picking out replicas in the gift shop, and while there's an admission fee for the museum, it's a lovely day out.

### Playlounge
*Soho, W1F 9RP*
Playlounge is just as much fun for adults as it is for children! The stock keeps design at the forefront with a focus on unique items, including many Japanese and manga items. There's a great range of action figures, cuddly toys and books, and it's a great place to find quirky toys.

Honeyjam

# Delectable
# Department Stores

**If you want to have a truly special shopping experience where service is second to none and the setting is as beautiful as the products on offer, pay a visit to one of London's high-end department stores.**

Liberty

### Liberty
*Regent Street, W1B 5AH*
Set in a Tudor building with wonderful architecture and offering a carefully chosen selection of high-end brands, Liberty is the ultimate in luxury shopping. It can be expensive but it's a very special shopping experience and perfect if you're looking for a unique designer item. Visit the haberdashery section to see the famous prints and fabrics, enjoy tea and cake in Café Liberty and buy some chocolates in the chocolate shop to get a coveted purple shopping bag.

### Selbys
*Holloway Road, N7 6PR*
One of the few truly independent department stores in the city, with charming and helpful staff, Selbys stocks everything from grapefruit knives to beds to a TopShop concession and a Caffè Nero.

### Harrods
*Knightsbridge, SW1X 7XL*
A visit to Harrods is an experience in itself, even if you don't buy anything! Harrods screams decadence from its seven food halls to the Egyptian room and the perfume hall. The huge range of departments means it really does live up to its motto of 'all things for all people, everywhere'. It can be very busy as it's a tourist hotspot but there are plenty of restaurants and cafés to escape to (including a Ladurée café selling the famous macaroons).

Harrods

**Tip**
Burlington Arcade is great for a special shopping trip. Built in 1819, the independent shops look like something out of a film and the arcade even has its own police force (the Beadles) to enforce the rules.

## Selfridges

*Oxford Street, W1A 1AB*
Voted the best department store in the world, Selfridges is shopping heaven. First plan some time to admire the 27 windows with their famous displays. Once inside you'll find six floors selling everything you could ever possibly need or want, with a great range of prices from high-end designers to high street favourites. The food hall is a must, with fun imported items like American cereals, and if shoes are your thing the shoe gallery will be like a dream come true.

## Heal's

*Tottenham Court Road, W1T 7LQ and other locations*
This furniture and home furnishings store has three branches across London but a visit to their flagship store on Tottenham Court Road is a must. Opened in 1840, Heal's sells a wonderful range of beautifully designed homeware items and the kitchen department has a fantastic array of tools and gadgets that make great gifts for aspiring cooks.

## Fortnum and Mason

*Green Park, W1A 1ER*
If you're looking for something special to eat, head to Fortnum and Mason. It's famous for its hampers, but you can browse the delicious items on offer and even enjoy a meal or afternoon tea at one of its five restaurants. There's more than just food, though: the upper floors offer clothes, homewares, luggage and all manner of lovely items including a specialist perfume range. This is a great place to come if you're looking for a gift (the tea selection is vast) and a visit offers a traditional and luxurious shopping experience.

Fortnum and Mason

> If I'm passing Fortnum and Mason on the hour I always stop to watch Mr Fortnum and Mr Mason come out of the clock to bow to each other.

# And Now for Something Completely Different . . .

## Specialist Stores

There are occasions when you need something a little bit special and London has a fantastic range of shops specialising in all manner of items from Beatles memorabilia to buttons and umbrellas.

### Davenports Magic
*Charing Cross, WC2N 4HZ*
The oldest family-run magic business in the world, Davenports is a treasure chest of magic treats that will excite young and old alike.

### The Beatles Store
*Marylebone, NW1 6XE*
With a huge range of memorabilia and branded items, from T-shirts, bags, mugs and magnets to autographed items, any Beatles fans will struggle not to empty their wallet! The shop is only about half an hour's walk from the Abbey Road studios, so you can make this a great addition to any Beatles tour.

The Beatles Store

### Angels Fancy Dress
*Shaftesbury Avenue, WC2H 8AE*
If you need a costume, look no further than Angels. With over 160 years' experience selling costumes, Angels offers hire costumes for a week and also stocks new costumes that are available to buy. There's a huge range of masks, make-up and wigs, so you're sure to find the perfect fancy dress outfit!

Davenports Magic

Viktor Wynd's Little Shop of Horrors

## Viktor Wynd's Little Shop of Horrors

*Hackney, E8 4RP*

A curiosity shop in Hackney run by the Last Tuesday Society, this really is the place to go for something weird and wonderful. Just browsing the peculiar items in this shop – including exorcism dolls and medical specimens in jars – is worth the £2 entry fee! Great if you are looking for something totally kooky and strange.

## Vx

*King's Cross, N1 9BT*

Vx (pronounced 'Vee-cross') is a vegan boutique, run by the Secret Society of Vegans, that sells food, clothing and books. Great if you are looking for vegan-friendly cakes, biscuits, ready meals and even pet food, the shop stocks a lot of specialist items that are hard to track down elsewhere.

## Blade Rubber Stamps

*Holborn, WC1A 2JL*

If you want to have a go at making your own cards or you're looking for a custom stamp, look no further. With reasonable prices and an incredible range of stamps the shop is a treasure trove of craft supplies.

## James Smith & Sons

*Tottenham Court Road, WC1A 1BL*

A wonderful shop that sells umbrellas from its traditional Victorian premises. Founded in 1830, this is still a family-run business and worth a visit just to look at the fantastic exterior.

## The Button Queen

*Marylebone, W1U 2PR*

The one-stop shop for all your button needs. From thousands of mother of pearl buttons to buttons adorned with plastic anchors, to beautiful glass buttons, you could spend hours perusing the stock.

## Gosh!

*Soho, W1F 0DR*

Laid out over two floors, Gosh! has a great selection of comics that will appeal to everyone from die-hard fans to newcomers. It stocks independent small press titles, manga and big names like DC and Marvel, and the enthusiastic staff are great at helping you find what you want.

James Smith & Sons

# Retro
# Heaven

## ■ Traid

*Brixton, SW2 5SG and other locations*
The various branches of Traid sell great vintage, high street and designer stock. Try to go when there's a sale on: everything is £4, then £3, then £2 and finally £1! A fabulous place to pick up a vintage bargain.

## ■ The East End Thrift Store

*Mile End, E1 4UT*
This retro clothing warehouse has a mix of vintage and remade clothing downstairs and a selection of carefully chosen and high-end vintage pieces upstairs. Everything is very reasonably priced, so you're sure to find something great.

**❝ I got some Marc Jacobs jeans for £2 and a Diane von Furstenberg dress for £3! ❞**

## ■ Beyond Retro

*Brick Lane, E2 6EJ and other locations*
The biggest East End warehouse for retro clothing, selling a great range of items from £15 dresses to tailored suits, Beyond Retro has everything, so be prepared to rummage! They also have a store in Soho.

## ■ Rokit

*Covent Garden, WC2H 9HZ, Brick Lane, E1 6SE and Camden, NW1 7BU*
With stores in Brick Lane, Camden and Covent Garden, there's always a great range of good-quality clothing for guys and gals – good for a quick dive in and a quirky find.

Traid

Rokit

## Shikasuki

*Primrose Hill, NW1 8LD*

A treasure trove of vintage pieces from Ossie Clark dresses to homewares, accessories and bags. Garments are rated according to quality and are organised by colour. This is a great place to have a rummage to find something truly special.

and you can find loads of unique pieces in a variety of styles.

## Blitz

*Brick Lane, E1 5JP*

A vintage department store off Brick Lane, Blitz is set in a Victorian warehouse. It sells everything from retro kitchenware, furniture and clothing to luggage and bikes.

> **The friendly staff at the East End Thrift Store even let me park my bike inside!**

## Hunky Dory

*Brick Lane, E1 6SA*

Hunky Dory won an award as best vintage shop in 2011 and with its great selection of clothes for men and women it's easy to see why. The items are always good quality and they have a wonderful range of accessories including handbags, hats, ties and shoes.

## Alfies Antique Market

*Lisson Grove, NW8 8DT*

A large indoor market with over 50 stalls selling a range of antique and retro items from jewellery, furniture and paintings to a brilliant selection of vintage clothing. There's also a rooftop café where you can enjoy lunch and admire your purchases.

## Mint

*Covent Garden, WC2 9LN*

With good-quality clothes spread across two levels, Mint stocks a great range of shoes, bags and other accessories on its lower level. There's plenty of choice for men and women,

Blitz

**Tip**

Vivien's of Holloway is the place to go if you're looking for a 1950s style dress. They do a great range of colours and prints in flattering styles – perfect if you're looking for a special outfit!

## The Vintage Emporium

*Brick Lane, E1 6LF*

Home to genuine vintage pieces (meaning they date from the Victorian era through to the 1950s), there's also a gorgeous tearoom upstairs.

**'TWO FOR A FIVER!'**

# Marvellous Markets

**London's many markets can be a great place to pick up a bargain – you can find anything from a comedy T-shirt to antique jewellery and fresh fruit and veg. As well as the ever-popular Camden and Portobello markets, make sure to spend some time wandering around these other great markets and their wonderful range of stalls.**

### ■ Haynes Lane Market
*Haynes Lane, Crystal Palace, SE19 3EN*
The place to go for vintage bargains, this market sells everything from vinyl records to books and toys, and it's great for clothes and jewellery. Finding the entrance can be confusing, but basically you get to the market through Westow Street and if you're coming from Crystal Palace High Street (Westow Hill), it's the first road on the right. There's normally a sign, but just ask if you get lost. The market is open on Tuesdays, Fridays, Saturdays and Sundays from 11am to 5pm.

### ■ Columbia Flower Market
*Columbia Road, Shoreditch, E2 7RG*
Get yourself down to Columbia Road on a Sunday to get a real taste of the East End. The market runs from 8am to 3pm every Sunday, though the road itself, a beautiful Victorian street with a rich history, is well worth a visit – it's lined with 60 independent boutiques. Most of the time it's quite quiet, but when the flower market is on it's a real bustle – shouts of 'three bunches a fiver' and customers stumbling around clutching bunches of gladioli all add to the buzzing atmosphere. If you get there when the barrow boys are packing up you can get some great deals.

### ■ Broadway Market
*Hackney, E8 4PH*
A smaller market than some, but still full of original clothing and accessories designed by local traders. The food is also great – a particular favourite is the roast beef and Yorkshire pudding sandwich! The market stalls are open on Saturdays so it's perfect for a Saturday afternoon stroll.

### ■ Greenwich Market
*Greenwich, SE10 9JA*
Greenwich Market is a brilliant place to go if you're looking for arts and crafts or unique antiques, with an emphasis on local and ethical designs. It's open seven days a week but at the weekend all the food stalls are open, selling gorgeous cupcakes, cheese and Italian lemonade.

Camden Passage

## Camden Passage

*Angel (just behind Upper Street),
N1 8ES*

Open on Wednesdays and Saturdays,
this is a small market selling vintage
clothes, furniture and jewellery. It's
located in a tiny, hidden street with
lovely clothes shops and cafés on
either side. You might have to scour
through lots of items to find a little
gem but the prices make it all
worthwhile.

## Spitalfields Market

*Liverpool Street, E1 6AA*

There are a whole host of independent
merchants and people who craft their

own quirky, beautiful products selling
their wares here. There's always some
gorgeous jewellery on offer as well
as some unique clothing items. The
market stalls are open Tuesday to Friday
10am to 4pm and from 9am to 5pm on
Sundays.

## Borough Market

*London Bridge, S1 1TL*

A huge food market next to Southwark
Cathedral that's open Thursday to
Saturday. A real foodie market with lots
of goodies, there are 130 stalls from a
number of countries including Portugal,
Argentina and Poland. Yummy chocolates, cheese, biscuits and loads of
places to buy lunch.

Cheese stand at Borough Market

## Petticoat Lane

*Liverpool Street, E1 7HT*

Known for leather goods and cut-price
fashion items, there are also some great
bric-a-brac stalls. The stalls are open
from Monday to Friday and on Sundays.
Remember to look for a Middlesex
Street sign and not one for Petticoat
Lane: the Victorians changed the name
because it was too naughty!

**Tip**

If you're in Spitalfields,
it's always worth
continuing on to Brick
Lane and swinging by
Brick Lane's Sunday
market for more of the
same but with a little more
of an independent feel.

# Independent Glory

# Beautiful Boutiques

### ■ Darkroom

*Russell Square, WC1N 3LL*

Darkroom is a concept store that prides itself on offering handmade, one-off products.  With a range including jewellery, scarves and art, this is a great place to visit for a unique purchase, perhaps from the next big-name designer.

### ■ Leila

*Muswell Hill, N10 3HN, Islington, N1 1RQ and Crouch End, N8 8PT*

Technically, this is a chain, but there are only three stores and they all sell amazing items. It's a great clothes shop with a variety of labels and some brilliant costume jewellery pieces.

Anthropologie

### ■ Bullfrogs

*Clapham Common, SW4 0JA and other locations*

A brilliant shoe and clothing store with a great range including vintage-inspired dresses and Converse trainers. There are a few bargains to be had with loads of top-quality products.

> **❝** I went to this amazing pet boutique and café called Verve in the heart of Notting Hill. The owners have a dog called Louie who is dripping in Swarovski crystals and wanders around the place in true rock star style! **❞**

### ■ Anthropologie

*Chelsea, SW3 4PW and Regent Street, W1B 5SW*

With beautiful dresses, lovely accessories and fabulous homewares, Anthropologie is like an Aladdin's cave of pretty things!

### ■ Precious

*Spitalfields, E1 7LJ*

A classic boutique stocking pieces from the likes of Moschino and Chloe. The styling service makes for a very special shopping experience.

### The Shop at Bluebird
*Chelsea, SW3 5UU*
A lifestyle store selling high-end items, the Shop at Bluebird is the place to go for hot new labels. It is laid out over 10,000 square feet and its innovative displays of their great range of clothes, homewares and coffee table books are constantly changing.

## ROCKING RECORDS
# Top Music Stores

### Rough Trade East
*Brick Lane, E1 6QL*
Some say that it's getting a little touristy, but the home of Rough Trade Records still has an incredible selection of music and in-store gigs. There's also a Rough Trade West store in Ladbroke Grove.

### BM Soho
*Soho, W1F 8EJ*
Specialising in club, house, drum and bass, dubstep and techno, BM Soho is home to an amazing selection of vinyl and some very knowledgeable staff who will help you explore the genre.

Rough Trade

### Haggle Vinyl
*Islington, N1 8LX*
A great independent store selling all manner of records from as little as £2. You can spend hours perusing the vast selection of records piled all over the store.

### Sister Ray
*Soho, W1F 8RP*
A large shop with a huge selection of records and CDs, and with helpful staff who are keen to help you find what you're looking for. They sell a great range of books, posters and T-shirts, and they also buy vinyl if you're looking to trim down your collection (but you'll probably increase it while you're there!)

### Revival
*Soho, W1F 8RH*
A great place to find rare or unusual records, Revival has a brilliant range of stock. They have a good jazz selection and if you take along your old stuff the staff will consider purchasing most items, including records, CDs and DVDs.

## LITERARY TREASURES

# Brilliant Bookshops

### ▪ Bookseller Crow on the Hill

*Crystal Palace, SE19 3AF*
The epitome of a wonderful local independent bookshop. The shop has a great range of titles and genres, and the staff are very willing to make suggestions. The owner writes a very popular blog and the shop also hosts a monthly book club. Pop in if you're looking for your next great read.

### ▪ Persephone Books

*Russell Square, WC1N 3NB*
Specialising in lost gems that were formerly out of print, this shop exclusively sells all of this independent publisher's list. The book design is divine, with grey covers and pretty end papers, which are different for each book and inspired by the content of the book, such as a material sample from the 1930s that the main character might have worn.

### ▪ Daunt Books

*Marylebone, W1U 4QW and other locations*
A gorgeous bookshop that arranges its books by country, so guides, maps, non-fiction and fiction all sit side by side in its Edwardian long oak galleries. An inspiration for any traveller or book lover. The various locations also host author events and a Walking Book Club.

### ▪ Foyles

*Charing Cross Road, WC2H 0EB*
With 200,000 books over five floors you would be hard pushed not to find what you are looking for here. Foyles

Daunt Books

also hosts year-round literary and music events.

### Tip

Cecil Court near Leicester Square is a treasure trove of specialist book stores.

### ▪ Under the Greenwood Tree

*Clapham Common, SW4 0JG*
A fantastic independent children's bookshop, Under the Greenwood Tree is home to friendly, knowledgeable staff who are happy to help or entertain the children while you browse through the wide selection of classic and contemporary books and beautiful toys. Story time is held every Saturday morning and there are fun activities for children throughout the school holidays.

Under the Greenwood Tree

**Tip**

London has lots of great secondhand bookshops, from the Oxfam bookshops in Bloomsbury and Marylebone to the fantastic range of quirky shops on Charing Cross Road.

## █ London Review Bookshop

*Holborn, WC1A 2JL*

This is a gem of an independent bookshop with knowledgeable staff and a fantastic coffee shop serving delicious cakes! It's a traditional bookshop that book lovers will adore, and the carefully considered stock selection means you're sure to find something you'll love to read while enjoying your coffee and cake.

## █ Hatchards

*Piccadilly, W1J 9LE*

This bookshop dates from 1797 and has a warm, comfortable feel about it. It may not be the biggest shop but it is a real treat to walk around looking at the staff recommendations.

## █ Stanfords

*Covent Garden, WC2E 9LP*

There are real gems to be found in this bookshop, established in 1853, which is reported to be the biggest travel bookshop in the world. The café is excellent as well.

## █ Black Gull Books

*Camden Lock Market, NW1 8AF*

A treasure trove of secondhand books which are stacked in piles all over the shop. It's a wonderful place to while away the hours searching through their diverse range of titles and it's a lovely break from the bustle of Camden High Street.

## █ Village Books

*Dulwich, SE21 7DE*

Full to the brim of a wonderful range of titles, this favourite in Dulwich village is often praised for the fact that the owners really make an effort to get to know their customers. It's a great place to go if you want some well-informed advice on what to read, from people who really know their stuff.

London Review Bookshop

# Chillingly Beautiful

# London's Cemeteries

**Although going for a walk or taking a guided tour around one of London's cemeteries may seem a little macabre, these historic spaces offer a fascinating insight into the rich past of the city.**

### Highgate Cemetery

*Highgate, N6 6PJ*
This Victorian cemetery is the final resting place of several famous people including George Eliot, Michael Faraday, Karl Marx and Douglas Adams. You can wander around the East Side independently but you need to go on a guided tour to see the West Side. The tours are very worthwhile if you want to learn all about the cemetery's fascinating history. It's a little spooky, but looking at all the incredible architecture is enjoyable and, despite its morbid purpose, the cemetery is a beautiful green space with lots of trees. It's especially nice in the autumn.

### Kensal Green

*Kensal Green, W10 4RA*
One of the oldest cemeteries in London, Kensal Green is also a nature reserve. It has 500 aristocratic 'residents' alongside the graves of Wilkie Collins, William Makepeace Thackeray and Isambard Kingdom Brunel. You can go on a tour to learn all about the history and stunning architecture and to see some of the 33 species of birds which reside here. The cemetery is free to visit and you can also buy a guide book pointing out the locations of the famous graves.

### Bunhill Fields

*Islington, EC1Y 1AU*
Originally used as a burial place for plague victims, Bunhill Fields was also used as a resting place for dissenters (16th–18th-century religious nonconformists). John Bunyan's tomb, an elaborate, stand-alone structure with scenes from his work *Pilgrim's Progress*, is a must-see. There are other famous graves, such as those of William Blake and Daniel Defoe, and you can either purchase a map showing their locations or go on a guided tour of this peaceful spot in the middle of the City.

> 66 Highgate is an unexpectedly calm and peaceful experience in the middle of a vibrant city. 99

## A FUN NIGHT OUT

# Bars with Retro Games

**If you're looking for a night out with a difference, why not try out a bar that offers the chance to play some retro games while you drink your beer?**

### The Old School Yard
*Borough, SE1 4PH*
A friendly, easy-going bar in Borough, this place is very relaxed, with people from all walks of life. Very retro, with a Foosball table and a Nintendo 64 with plenty of old-school games, there's also a karaoke room. The cocktails are brilliant and happy hour is every night between 5.30pm and 8pm.

Table football at Bar Kick

### Bar Kick
*Shoreditch, E1 6JE*
A fun place to go for a drink, not only is this a great place to watch football on widescreen TVs, you can even indulge in a bit of the beautiful game yourself on one of their several football tables. There's a great atmosphere once the tables get busy and you could find yourself in the middle of a mini tournament.

### Bloomsbury Lanes
*Euston, WC1H 9EU*
This is a great place for a birthday party or a unique night out. There's bowling, karaoke booths, great cocktails and yummy burgers, and the lanes stay open until late. Later on it becomes a bit of a dancing spot and once the music starts those bowling shoes work wonders as dancing shoes!

### The Book Club
*Shoreditch, EC2A 4RH*
A very trendy bar with great music and dancing, the cool thing about this place is the ping-pong tables. The tables are free to use and are really good fun!

> ❝ The Namco Centre at Waterloo is a really fun place for a night out — bowling, bumper cars and all the arcade games you could want! ❞

# Art and Culture

London is renowned for its cultural offerings – be it cutting-edge art, incredible theatre, great live music, stunning architecture or gorgeous independent cinemas, there's so much on offer that it can sometimes be hard to choose what to see and do next. We've come up with our favourite cultural activities and fun nights out to help you enjoy all the city has to offer.

**UNMISSABLE**

# Galleries and Museums

### ■ Sir John Soane's Museum
*Holborn, WC2A 3BP*
The museum showcases one man's eccentric collection of art from the 18th to the 19th century. You walk through the rooms of his home, which are stuffed with a wide variety of objects from Roman, Greek and Egyptian antiquity. And it's free, to boot. Try to go along to their monthly evening candle tours on the first Tuesday of the month.

### ■ Victoria and Albert Museum
*South Kensington, SW7 2RL*
The Victoria and Albert Museum (V&A) was built to showcase British design and manufacturing. The collection is a celebration of decorative and applied arts and includes displays of jewellery, fashion, sculpture, ceramic works, photographs and metalwork.

### ■ Tate Modern
*Southwark, SE1 9TG*
Wild and wacky art as you've never seen it before. A stunning architectural space with fantastic views over the Thames and the Millennium Bridge make this a great space to wander about.

### ■ National Gallery
*Trafalgar Square, WC2N 5DN*
Set aside a day and enjoy some of the best art in the world dating from the 13th to the 20th century, from Botticelli and Titian to Constable, Turner and Van Gogh.

## ■ Hunterian Museum

*Holborn, WC2A 3PE*
The Hunterian Museum is not for the squeamish! It houses the collection of the 18th-century surgeon and anatomist John Hunter and contains over 3,000 specimens, including organs  in jars and anatomical displays. Not the place to go straight after lunch, but the displays are fascinating nonetheless and worth a visit.

## ■ Wallace Collection

*Marylebone, W1U 3BN*
This museum is a joy with a collection that includes suits of armour, old master paintings and ceramics. Lift the covers on the cabinets and marvel at the miniature portraits.

## ■ Imperial War Museum

*Lambeth North, SE1 6HZ*
A fantastic museum if you have any interest in war and its machinery. Look out for special exhibitions and visit the First World War trenches and the Second World War air raid shelter simulator.

## ■ Museum of London, Docklands

*Canary Wharf, E14 4AL*
Located in one of the original warehouses that the museum celebrates and charting the history of London as a port, the museum contains some wonderful exhibits.

## ■ Tate Britain

*Pimlico, SW1P 4RG*
Sometimes overshadowed by its trendy sister museum the Tate Modern, the Tate Britain has the most brilliant collection of British paintings. The building itself is beautiful and the chance to see works by such names as Constable and Turner is an opportunity you shouldn't miss.

**Tip**
There is a boat service that runs between the Tate Britain and the Tate Modern. It's a lovely day out exploring both of the galleries and enjoying a trip up the Thames in between.

## ■ The Wellcome Collection

*Euston, NW1 2BE*
Exhibiting a collection of medical artefacts and other regularly changing exhibits, the Wellcome Collection is small enough to see everything in one visit, and entry is free.

## ■ Royal Academy

*Piccadilly, W1J 0BD*
Located in a beautiful part of London, the building itself is stunning and the exhibitions are always interesting and thought-provoking. If you can, it makes sense to become a member as you get free entry to all the exhibitions and you can enjoy the 'Friends' Room', a delightful little coffee shop.

## ■ Museum of London

*Barbican, EC2Y 5HN*
A great museum tracing the history of London from Roman times, with excellent interactive displays. The perfect place to come if you want to learn more about the history of the city.

# And Action!
# Six Famous Film Locations

### Priory Church of St Bartholomew the Great
*Farringdon, EC1A 9DS*
This beautiful church has featured in quite a few films. Most famously, it was Nottingham Cathedral in *Robin Hood: Prince of Thieves*, the church where Joseph Fiennes begs for forgiveness in *Shakespeare in Love* and, a real British favourite, the church where Charles gets punched by Duckface in *Four Weddings and a Funeral*. Well worth a visit!

### Borough Market
*Southwark, SE1 1TL*
The film adaptation of the much-loved novel shows perennial singleton Bridget Jones living in a flat above the Globe pub in trendy Borough Market. The market was also used in *Lock, Stock and Two Smoking Barrels.*

### 33 Portland Place
*Marylebone, W1B 1QE*
This Georgian townhouse became the consulting room of speech therapist Lionel Logue in the Oscar-winning film *The King's Speech*. You might also recognise the shabby chic interior from Amy Winehouse's *Rehab* music video.

### The Salisbury
*Harringay, N4 1JX*
This Grade II listed pub has been used in numerous films, including *Spider* by

David Cronenburg, and served as Fagan's pub in *The Long Good Friday.*

### King's Cross Station
*King's Cross, N1 9AP*
Head to King's Cross for a great photo opportunity. You can pose with a luggage trolley disappearing into the wall at this iconic *Harry Potter* location.

Platform 9¾ at King's Cross

### Farmiloe Building
*Farringdon EC1 M4BE*
This Victorian warehouse building has been used in several film and television productions, serving as a Russian restaurant in *Eastern Promises,* has featured in *Sherlock Holmes* with Robert Downey Jr and was chosen by Christopher Nolan as the location for the Gotham City Police headquarters in his Batman films.

## TREADING THE BOARDS FURTHER AFIELD

# Theatres Outside the West End

**The area around Shaftesbury Avenue might be known as Theatreland, but we've looked a bit further afield and put together a list of fabulous theatres outside the West End.**

### Shakespeare's Globe

*Southwark, SE1 9DT*

The home of the Bard! Whether you are standing with the groundlings or lording it in the stalls, this amazing and authentic venue enables audiences to watch Shakespeare's plays the way they were meant to be seen.

### Orange Tree Theatre

*Richmond, TW9 2SA*

London's only permanent theatre in the round, the Orange Tree is a fantastic smaller theatre with historical significance. It garnered fame for providing a venue for the revolutionary Czech poet and politician Václav Havel during the years of Communist repression.

### National Theatre

*Waterloo, SE1 9PX*

Home to three performance spaces, the National Theatre is housed within ultra-modern architecture and offers a wonderful range of shows. They do great student deals and £5 tickets if you're under 26.

### Old Vic Tunnels

*Waterloo, SE1 8SW*

Run by the Old Vic, the Old Vic Tunnels is a performance space with a difference.

Located in an old coal store underneath Waterloo station, it's a very atmospheric space and a unique theatre experience.

### Lyric Hammersmith

*Hammersmith, W6 0QL*

The modern exterior of this theatre belies its historical interior. There are two performance venues: the main stage is a 19th-century space, while the smaller studio is home to productions by up-and-coming companies. There's also a lovely roof garden where you can enjoy a drink or a meal before the show.

**Tip**
The terrace bar at the National has some lovely views over the Thames towards the London Eye, making it a really pretty place to enjoy a drink.

# Rocking Out

# London's Best Live Music Venues

### ■ The Half Moon

*Putney, SW15 1EU*

A famous venue because of its prestigious guests back in the 1970s, the Half Moon still plays host to a large variety of bands and acts in its custom venue space. The venue is an intimate and atmospheric room which brings you really close to the act and lets you really feel the music.

### ■ The Crobar

*Tottenham Court Road, W1D 4AS*

A great place to 'rock out' in the evening. Open from 4pm to 4am and featuring heavy metal music and beer in cans. What more could you ask for?

### ■ Monto Water Rats

*King's Cross, WC1X 8BZ*

This tiny, iconic venue is an ordinary pub during the day but it's known as the place to see up-and-coming bands in London and its small size makes gigs really intimate.

### ■ Bull and Gate

*Kentish Town, NW5 2TJ*

An Irish pub with an intimate gig space in the back, the Bull and Gate mostly offers rock and indie music, but it's bigger than it looks from the outside and has a great atmosphere with brilliant acoustics.

> 66 The massive disco ball in Koko is the largest in Europe — I love admiring it! 99

### ■ KOKO

*Mornington Crescent, NW1 7JE*

A former theatre and cinema, KOKO became a music venue in the 1970s and quickly became the place for seminal performances, entering music history with gigs by the Sex Pistols, the Clash, the Cure, Madonna and Coldplay. It still manages to feel intimate despite its multiple levels, and the varying levels mean that you can try out different views and choose the one that suits you best. There's a bar on each level, so you won't need to go far to get a drink.

KOKO

## The Electric Ballroom

*Camden Town, NW1 8QP*
Located right next to Camden Town station, the Electric Ballroom might seem a little run-down now, but that's just part of its charm. A great place for live music, and it also runs club nights at the weekend.

## HMV Forum

*Kentish Town, NW5 1JY*
The HMV Forum was once an art deco cinema and its multiple bars and balcony area, along with the main floor, make it a great place to see live music.

## Ronnie Scott's

*Soho, W1D 4HT*
A jazz institution but not overly done up for tourists or excessively expensive. There's a great atmosphere with brilliant performances by guest artists and the house band.

## Union Chapel

*Highbury and Islington, N1 2XD*
Union Chapel is one of the most unique places for live music in London. It's a functioning chapel on Sundays, but during the week you can choose a pew and admire the stunning architecture while appreciating the great acoustics as you listen to the music. This is a large venue

Jose James at Ronnie Scott's

Union Chapel

which also does special film screenings, such as the classic *Dracula* at Hallowe'en.

## 100 Club

*Tottenham Court Road, W1D 1LL*
One of London's most iconic live music venues, where acts such as the Rolling Stones and Paul McCartney have graced the stage, this is an absolute must-visit for any rock, blues or jazz fan!

## O2 Academy

*Brixton, SW9 9SL*
This old theatre building has been a central part of the live music and clubbing scene for decades, and big acts from all genres of music perform here. It's very grand inside and because the floor slopes, even short people can see the stage in a busy crowd!

## 229

*Marylebone, W1W 5PN*
An intimate little underground venue that is particularly good for rock and metal gigs.

## Proud

*Camden Town, NW1 8AH*
Great venue that has a wide variety of indie bands and DJs performing. It can get very busy at the weekend, so get there early!

## STANDING TALL

# Favourite Statues

If you start to look for them you'll notice that London is full of beautiful and interesting statues. Whether they're dedicated to a great leader or just a nod to a beloved character, London's statues all add to the character of the city.

### Queen Alexandra

*Opposite Marlborough House, SW1A 1DD*
Usually overlooked by the hordes of tourists watching the Changing of the Guard, this rare example of an art nouveau statue was designed by Alfred Gilbert, more famous for his Eros statue in Piccadilly Circus.

### Samuel Johnson's cat

*Gough Square, EC4A 3DE*
This cute statue of Samuel Johnson's cat Hodge includes some oyster shells, as oysters were Hodge's favourite food.

### Battle of Britain Monument

*Victoria Embankment, SW1A*
Make sure to walk around this sculpture several times; it depicts the people who helped win the Battle of Britain and each time you will find different things to look at. Look out for the man trying to steal a kiss!

### Albert Memorial

*Kensington Gardens, SW7*
A stunning monument to love and loss, this memorial was commissioned by Queen Victoria to commemorate her beloved husband Prince Albert. It is magnificent and even on a dull day it sparkles and glows.

### Peter Pan

*Kensington Gardens, W2*
Originally commissioned by J. M. Barrie himself as a May Day gift to the children of London, George Frampton's beautiful, elfin sculpture of the boy who never grew up will always make you smile.

### Paddington Bear

*Paddington Station, W2 1HQ*
Complete with his battered suitcase, this charming rustic-style statue of Paddington gives the impression that he has just wandered off a train from deepest, darkest Peru.

### Achilles

*Hyde Park, SW7*
Officially commemorating the Duke of Wellington's military victories, the statue of Achilles in Hyde Park has become more  famous for its fig leaf, which was added by the Victorians to spare ladies' blushes.

### Roosevelt and Churchill

*Between Old and New Bond Streets, W1S*

Called 'Allies', the bronze replicas of Roosevelt and Churchill commemorate 50 years of peace after the Second World War. This is a fun photo opportunity as you can join the two great leaders for a seat as they relax on their bench.

# Good for a Laugh
# Cracking Comedy Clubs

### Leicester Square Theatre

*Leicester Square, WC2H 7BX*

A great place to watch comedy, the theatre has a constantly revolving guest list of prestigious comedians and up-and-coming acts. The venue has two bars at either side of the seating, so it's easy to get a drink while you're enjoying the show.

### Bearcat Comedy Club

*Twickenham, TW1 1LF*

An excellent night of laughter. This is where all the stars start off before they get big. It's great value for money and a really intimate venue to see some great stand-up.

### Comedy Store

*Leicester Square, SW1Y 4EE*

The breeding ground for so many great comics, the Comedy Store is something of an institution. With stand-up and improv nights by the Comedy Store Players, you're guaranteed a good laugh. This is also a great place to see comics fine-tuning their acts for the Edinburgh Festival.

### 99 Club

*Islington, EC1V 1NQ and other locations*

The 99 Club has been awarded several 'best comedy club' titles by critics from several different sources and so is known as the London critics' choice. There's comedy every night of the week at their various venues and you can even have a meal before the show.

### Comedy Carnival

*Leicester Square, WC2H 7NG and Clapham Junction, SW11 1TT*

With shows every week (on Fridays in Leicester Square and on Saturdays in the Clapham Grand), the Comedy Carnival is consistently praised for its brilliant line-ups. They always deliver a great night and have played host to some big names like Michael McIntyre, Micky Flanagan and Sarah Millican. At the Clapham Grand your ticket allows you to stay and enjoy the night-club after the show ends!

## MARVELLOUS MASTERPIECES

# Must-See Paintings

With its superb range of galleries and museums housing some of the most sensational works of art, London is a paradise for art appreciation. We've put together our list of the absolute must-see works of art on show in the city – you'd be a fool to miss them.

### John Singer Sargent: *Carnation, Lily, Lily, Rose*

*Tate Britain, SW1P 4RG*
Painted over a series of evenings during 1885 and 1886. Sargent painted for short bursts of time at twilight each evening when the light level was just right. The painting shows the daughter of the artist's friend, and the length of time required to complete the painting was certainly worth it as the use of colour and light and shade evokes a harmonious summer's evening.

**Tip**

The National Portrait Gallery Portrait Award is an annual competition that is shown over the summer. Anyone can enter a portrait, including untrained artists. The best entries are displayed in the gallery and range from massive, detailed and lifelike paintings to more abstract interpretations.

### Vincent Van Gogh: *Sunflowers*

*National Gallery, WC2N 5DN*
Although it appears on so many things, from mouse mats to teacloths, there is still nothing like standing in front of the real thing, admiring the use of colour.

### Henri Matisse: *The Snail*

*Tate Britain, SW1P 4RG*
This large, colourful spiral was created while Matisse was unwell, which meant that he had to direct an assistant to position the paper shapes painted with gouache. Once Matisse was happy with the placement, the paper was glued down. One of Matisse's later works, its simple colours and shapes are stunning.

### John Constable: *The Hay Wain*

*National Gallery, WC2N 5DN*
A hay wain is a type of cart, which in this painting is shown in the River

The Hay Wain

Stour in Suffolk. Typical of Constable's Arcadian landscapes, this painting is now one of the most iconic of Constable's pictures of the English countryside. It's wonderful to stand and admire it, losing yourself in his wonderful clouds.

### ■ Joseph Turner: *The Fighting Temeraire*

*National Gallery, WC2N 5DN*
This painting shows Turner at his best, commenting on the passing of the majesty of tall sailing ships and the change to steam. Take some time to admire his wonderful glowing sky.

### ■ Hogarth: *A Rake's Progress*

*Sir John Soane's Museum, WC2A 3BP*
Hogarth's eight paintings show the series of events leading to the downfall of a young man, Tom Rakewell, in London. The series features scenes in a brothel and a gambling house and includes historic London locations such as the Fleet debtors' prison and Bedlam Hospital.

**TIP**

If you only want to see just one painting collection in London, check out the Turner Galleries at the Tate Britain – quintessentially English!

### ■ Georges Seurat: *Bathers at Asnières*

*National Gallery, WC2N 5DN*
This large work uses simple forms and regular shapes to depict a group of

Bathers at Asnières

workmen relaxing by the banks of the Seine. Seurat had not yet invented his famous pointillist technique, but he did later rework parts of the painting using this technique, confirming the work's place as one of his early masterpieces.

### ■ Lucas Cranach: *Adam and Eve*

*The Courtauld Institute of Art, WC2R 0RN*
Cranach's painting, which shows the serpent watching Eve offer the apple to Adam, is admired for its careful attention to detail, in both the animals (including a unicorn and a deer regarding its reflection in a pool) and in its depiction of the nude human form.

### ■ Hackney Peace Carnival Mural

*Hackney, E8 3BG*
One of London's largest and most colourful murals, this is a great example of street art.

### ■ George Stubbs: *Whistlejacket*

*National Gallery, WC2N 5DN*
This painting by George Stubbs is so lifelike you wouldn't be surprised if he jumped off the canvas and galloped away!

# Picture Postcard
# London Landmarks

## ■ Hammersmith Bridge
*On the A306, SE1*

A lesser-known but beautiful bridge over the Thames, this suspension bridge dates from 1887 and is a Grade II listed structure.

## ■ Natural History Museum
*South Kensington, SW7 5BD*

Often described as the 'Cathedral of Nature', the Natural History Museum opened in 1881. The museum is built in a Romanesque style with blue and cream terracotta tiles covering the walls. Intricate sculptures of various plants and animals decorate the exterior walls, featuring all sorts of species, both living and extinct. The stunning architecture continues inside with high ceilings, a huge staircase and beautifully carved pillars.

## ■ Monument
*Fish Street Hill, EC3R 6DB*

Erected to commemorate the Great Fire of London in 1666, the monument is a stone Doric column designed by Christopher Wren. You can climb the 311 stairs to the top for incredible views of London. The height of the column marks the distance to where the fire started in Pudding Lane: if you laid the monument down (in the right direction) it would reach the spot where the fire began.

## ■ O2 Arena
*North Greenwich, SE10 0DX*

The O2 Arena could have been iconic for the wrong reasons. Once the ill-fated Millennium Dome, the venue's reputation was transformed in 2007 when it opened as an entertainment venue. The design of the dome, with its white marquee and support towers, has now become an attraction in itself. You can climb across the roof to a viewing platform at the very top and see how this iconic venue is a part of the Greenwich skyline.

## ■ Tower Bridge
*Tower Hill, SE1*

Such a landmark that you almost don't notice it any more, it is definitely worth taking a moment to stop and admire Tower Bridge. The bridge still opens (you can check the timetable online) and you can even admire the view from the exhibition at the top of the bridge.

## ■ Battersea Power Station
*Battersea, SW8 5BP*

One of London's most iconic buildings, it is far from a visitor's attraction as you can't actually get in. Still, it dominates  the London skyline and is easily recognisable for anyone who gets the train to Waterloo!

# Al Fresco
# Top Outdoor Theatre and Cinema

### ■ Opera Holland Park

*Kensington, W8 6LU*
Set in a specially erected tent in the
middle of the park, Opera Holland
Park puts on a summer season of shows
ranging from classics like *Così Fan Tutte* to
*Fantastic Mr Fox*.

### ■ Somerset House

*Westminster, WC2R 1LA*
Every summer the courtyard at
Somerset House is home to a 12-day film
programme featuring a range of movies
from new art house offerings to classics
like *Die Hard*. There are no chairs, but
you can take a picnic and soak up the
atmosphere before settling down to
enjoy the film.

### ■ Regent's Park Outdoor Theatre

*Queen Mary's Garden, Regent's Park,
NW1 4NY*
Open from May to September every
year, this is a unique theatre-going
experience set in the heart of Regent's
Park. You can take a picnic along, sit in
the stands and soak up the atmosphere
of live, outdoor theatre, film or comedy,
with performances of plays such as *Lord
of the Flies* and *A Midsummer Night's Dream*.

### ■ The Scoop

*London Bridge, SE1 2DB*
An outdoor amphitheatre on the banks
of the Thames next to City Hall, the
Scoop hosts some wonderful outdoor
events. With a capacity of 800 people,
the Scoop puts on a programme of free
events including film, music and theatre.
Seats are allocated on a first-come
first-served basis, but you can take in
food. There's no cover, so make sure you
dress for any weather!

Regent's Park Theatre

### Tip

The Secret Cinema (www.
secretcinema.org) is a
members-only event that
stages screenings in
interesting places which
relate to the film they're
showing. It could be
outside, it could be in an
old vault – it could be
anywhere!

69

# The Kids Are Alright

# Top Activities for Children in London

**It can make you see London in a whole new light when you see it through a child's eyes. Here's our pick of some events and activities that kids will love.**

## City farms
*Various locations*
All over the city, from Mudchute to Hounslow, most city farms have free entry and are a great rural experience in an urban environment. Some are quite big, others pretty tiny, but they all provide wonderful oases in the bustling city. Particular favourites are the centrally located Vauxhall City Farm, which has both small animals (guinea pigs and enormous rabbits) and larger animals like horses (the farm also runs subsidised riding lessons), goats and alpaca. The Woodlands Farm, a small and welcoming farm in southeast London, is also worth a visit as it runs a few special events throughout the year which are perfect for the whole family. Lambing day at Woodlands is lovely as children are encouraged to meet and stroke the newborn lambs and there are crafts, activities and homemade cake!

## Bunny Park
*Hanwell, W7 3BP*
A small zoo with a sweet playground and café, Bunny Park is very popular with 2–8-year-olds and it's all free! The zoo is home to monkeys, mongooses, goats and parrots. There's also a maze made up of 2,000 yew trees.

Mudchute City Farm

## Kew Bridge Steam Museum

*Kew, TW8 0EN*

With a low entry fee, this is a great place to take kids on a day out. You can see working steam engines and they also have specialist model railway days. They also run a steam train on the outdoor track.

## The Big Draw

*Various locations*

Taking place in October at various locations across London, this event gives children the chance to learn from artists, whatever age they are. With workshops by illustrators, product designers, architects or fashion designers, this is a great way of letting kids express their creative side.

## IMAX cinema

*Waterloo, SE1 8XR*

A film at the IMAX cinema is a great way to round off a day at the South Bank. The screen at the BFI Imax is 80ft high (that's five double decker buses!) and kids will love seeing blockbusters like *Harry Potter* or watching nature documentaries in 3D on a screen four times larger than normal.

## Lollibop Festival

*Regent's Park, NW1 4NR*

Known as 'The Big Bash for Little Kids', Lollibop is a festival designed especially for children under 10 and their families

that takes place over a few days in August. Full of fun-packed activities, story time and favourite book and television characters, Lollibop is certainly one for the parent's calendar!

## Harry Potter locations

Any Harry Potter fan will love visiting locations used in the books and films:

- Leadenhall Market – entrance to the Leaky Cauldron

- King's Cross Station – Platform 9¾

- Foyer of Australia House – Gringotts Bank

- St Pancras Station – Harry and Ron fly by in Mr Weasley's car

- Great Scotland Yard – entrance to Ministry of Magic

- Westminster Underground Station – Harry and Mr Weasley get stuck in the ticket barriers

- River Thames – Harry and the Order of the Phoenix travel up the river on broomsticks

- Millennium Bridge – the bridge is attacked by the Death Eaters.

- Reptile House at London Zoo – in *Harry Potter and the Philosopher's Stone* Harry Speaks to a snake before accidentally setting it free and trapping his cousin Dudley in the display instead.

Take them on a black cab ride — my boys loved it!

## MORE THAN ANCIENT POTTERY HERE

# Unusual Museums

**If you're looking for a more unique museum experience or just want to learn more about a specialised topic, pay a visit to one of London's more unusual museums.**

### ▪ Old Operating Theatre Museum and Herb Garret

*Southwark, SE1 9RY*

A real unexpected treat, even getting in and out is an adventure with access up a steep, winding staircase. Telling the history of surgery in a surviving operating theatre, the exhibition is fascinating, but try to go when there's a demonstration on.

### ▪ Museum of Childhood

*Bethnal Green, E2 9PA*

The Museum of Childhood is open seven days a week and entry is free. The museum is located in a beautiful Victorian building with a glass ceiling, meaning that it's always flooded with natural light. It's the perfect place for children to get excited (and parents to get nostalgic) about toys – anything from hobby horses to Tamagotchis.

### ▪ Grant Museum of Zoology

*Euston Square, WC1E 6DE*

This is a fabulous space crammed with fascinating zoological specimens, from tiny sea corals to alligators. Housed in an old medical library, the exhibits are contained in beautiful display cases and floor-to-ceiling heavy wood shelves. Despite its small size there is so much to see that an hour slips by very quickly!

### ▪ Foundling Museum

*Camden Town, WC1N 1AZ*

The Foundling Museum tells the story of Britain's first home for abandoned children, outlining a fascinating history of the work of the hospital in caring for the children and the story of the three founders: philanthropist Thomas Coram, the composer Handel and the artist Hogarth. The museum is also home to an impressive art collection and has a lovely park for children to play in.

> ❝ The café at the Museum of Childhood is a great place to read – and they do really good cake! ❞

## ■ Museum of Brands, Advertising and Packaging

*Ladbroke Grove, W11 2AR*
Dedicated to everything about branding, packaging and advertising, this museum is a must for anyone in this field, or for those who fancy feeling a bit nostalgic as they recognise packaging from their childhood. From toys, food products and games to memorabilia from every era, this museum is a great way to explore the past through labels.

## ■ Cinema Museum

*Elephant and Castle, SE11 4TH*
Celebrating the evolution of cinemas in Britain, this museum offers a great insight into the days before huge multiplexes, keeping alive the spirit of the picture house in the modern age. Book ahead, as places on tours need to be reserved.

Grade II listed building that houses the museum. The museum has a great gift shop and even holds fan-making workshops.

## ■ London Canal Museum

*King's Cross, N1 9RT*
Charting the story of London's canals, this museum has displays on the people, horses and boats that were

involved in this once-thriving trade. The history of the ice trade these boats served is fascinating and it's really interesting exploring a narrow boat cabin and the former ice warehouse in which the museum is housed.

## ■ Twinings Museum

*Westminster, WC2R 1AP*
The Twinings Museum charts the

❝ My vote would be for the Imperial War Museum. Possibly the best playground for grown-ups — nothing beats climbing inside a WWII Halifax bomber, sitting down in the bombadier's seat and saying, 'Bombs away!' ❞

## ■ Fan Museum

*Greenwich, SE10 8ER*
The first museum in the world dedicated to fans, this museum has over 3,500 fans dating from the 11th century to the present day. You can learn all about the history of fans, and how they are made, all while admiring the 18th-century

history of the Twinings family and their association with the traditional British brew. There are some great artefacts, such as vintage packaging and special edition tea caddies, and in the shop next door you can taste and buy tea from the wide range of Twinings products.

# Simply the Best Silver Screens

## Independent Cinemas

### ■ Prince Charles Cinema
*Leicester Square, WC2H 7BY*
This gem, just off Leicester Square, hosts a variety of cult screenings and fun events revolving around popular films. They really care about film and film fans, and in particular, they are very good about taking suggestions and communicating with their audience via social media.

### ■ The Aubin Cinema
*Shoreditch, E2 7DP*
Downstairs cinema owned by Shoreditch House, good for a more personal and lavish film viewing! You can recline on your very own sofa while watching a film with a bottle of wine from the bar.

### ■ Lexi Cinema
*Kensal Rise, NW10 3JU*
Run by volunteers, the Lexi Cinema not only runs community-friendly screenings for children, senior citizens, film clubs, etc., but it also donates 100% of its profits to charity. Brings a whole new meaning to feel-good films.

### ■ The Phoenix Cinema
*East Finchley, N2 9PJ*
A classic 1930s cinema showing the latest independent and foreign films. It's also been used as a backdrop to *Black Books, Interview with the Vampire* and *Nowhere Boy.*

### ■ Screen on the Green
*Islington, N1 0NP*
A great 1950s cinema with just a single screen but a fantastic programme of British films and cult classics – there's always a queue, but once you're in just relax on the sofas and enjoy.

### ■ Rich Mix
*Shoreditch, E1 6LA*
Shows a great mix of general release films as well as plenty of art house, independent, world films and documentaries.

### ■ The Electric Cinema
*Ladbroke Grove, W11 2ED*
A piece of cinematic history in its own right, the Electric Cinema has survived in Portobello Road for over 100 years. Packed with leather seats and footstools, tables for food and drink and even two-seater sofas at the back, it really feels like a home from home . . . with a massive screen!

**Tip**
Film lovers should head to Arthur's on the Green in Twickenham for one of their movie nights. They have a set menu and they even match the food to the chosen film!

# I Could Have Danced All Night

# Places to Go Dancing

### ▌ The Tram and Social

*Tooting Broadway, SW17 9NA*
Set in an old tram shed with high
ceilings and quirky retro décor (floral
wallpaper and kitsch artefacts), it's free
to get in with a *huge* selection of bottled
beers from every corner of the globe.
Amazing music of all genres: pop, indie,
folk, soul, blues, new stuff and old
stuff – but all songs that make you
want to get up and dance. They're
open until 2am so you have plenty of
time to enjoy the music.

### ▌ Bethnal Green Working Men's Club

*Bethnal Green, E2 6NB*
Great for a quirky night, with 1950s
prom evenings, games nights where you
get your takeaway delivered and jailhouse
rock evenings complete with mugshots
and whisky.

### ▌ Mahiki

*Mayfair, W1S 4LD*
You'll catch a
glimpse of some
of the royals here!
It's the best club
for celeb spotting,
but go armed with
your credit card as
it's very pricey!

### ▌ Embargo 59

*Fulham Broadway, SW10 0TZ*
Stylish with great cocktails, it's not very
well known yet so you won't have a huge
queue to contend with!

### ▌ Funky Buddha

*Green Park, W1J 8DY*
Great atmosphere and people, this is a
more intimate club that's famous on the
London club circuit.

### ▌ Egg

*Camden, N7 9AX*
An amazing venue with an outdoor
terrace and garden, there's even a
swimming pool in the summer!

### ▌ Pacha

*Victoria, SW1V 1JR*
A huge dance floor and a great
atmosphere. You can book tickets in
advance, so getting in isn't a problem.
One of the better clubs for house and
garage music.

### ▌ Zoo Bar

*Leicester Square, WC2H 7AQ*
Less expensive than normal London
clubs, the crazy retro décor is part of
the charm. It's always lively and full, and
they do half-price drinks before 9pm.

# Literary Locations

London has a rich literary history as the home to numerous great names and as the inspiration and setting for countless poems, novels and plays. Here are a few must-see literary locations, as well as a few lesser-known ones, to inspire your inner bookworm.

## Must-See

### ■ The Sherlock Holmes Museum

*Baker Street, NW1 6XE*

The address of one of the most famous literary detectives, 221b Baker Street is now a museum dedicated to Arthur Conan Doyle's Sherlock Holmes. Set up as a reconstruction of the fictional house where many mysteries were solved, it is a fun way to explore the novels and you may even have Holmes himself showing you round!

### ■ The Charles Dickens Museum

*Russell Square, WC1N 2LX*

The home of Charles Dickens from 1837 to 1839, the house is now a museum

The Charles Dickens Museum

**Tip**
Dr Johnson's House is near to the Dickens Museum, if you're interested in where the first comprehensive English dictionary was written.

dedicated to the writer. It's truly fantastic to see Dickens' manuscripts and his study and to be in the place where *Oliver Twist* and *The Pickwick Papers* were created. A few streets away is Lincoln's Inn Hall, which features in the famous opening to *Bleak House*.

### ■ Keats House

*Hampstead, NW3 2RR*

The museum at the house where Keats lived from 1818 to 1820 is a great way to learn more about the man behind such ethereal poetry. The house has been beautifully restored so that you can see the rooms where Keats and his friend Charles Brown lived, as well as the rooms of the adjoining house where Keats met and fell in love with Fanny

Brawne. The rooms where Keats lived and worked give a wonderful insight into the poet's life and walking in the beautiful garden you can see why he was inspired to write such beautiful poetry.

# Lesser-Known

### ■ Rules Restaurant
*Covent Garden, WC2E 7LB*
If you visit Rules, the oldest restaurant in London, you'll be eating in the same place as Arthur Conan Doyle, and you can still order the same traditional English food (like steak and kidney pudding) that he enjoyed.

### ■ The sole remaining wall of the Marshalsea Debtors' Prison
*Borough, SE1 1JA*
A poignant reminder of south London's poverty, the Marshalsea Debtors' Prison inspired Dickens in a profoundly personal way. When his father was imprisoned here in 1824, the 12-year-old Dickens was forced to leave school and work in a factory to support his family.

### ■ Putney Bridge
*Putney Bridge on the A219, SW15*
A walk across Putney Bridge not only gives wonderful views of the Thames and the rowing clubs dotted along the banks; it also allows you to reflect on a pivotal moment in literary history. In 1795 the radical women's writer Mary Wollstonecraft tried to commit suicide by jumping from the bridge. She was saved by passers-by, though, and went on to marry William Godwin, with whom she had a daughter, Mary Shelley.

## Tip
If you're in Putney, stop by Festing Road. You'll see a paving stone commemorating the fact that the illustrator David McKee lived at number 54 and that his creation, Mr Benn, lived at number 52.

Remaining wall of Marshalsea Debtors' Prison

### ■ The home of the author of Mary Poppins
*50 Smith Street, Chelsea, SWZ 4EP*
The Australian actress and author P.L. Travers took inspiration from her street in Chelsea for Cherry Tree Lane, the home of Jane and Michael Banks in her first novel in the Mary Poppins series. Travers later sent a photograph of the front door to Walt Disney when he was making his film adaptation.

# Open Spaces and Sport

London is a huge city: a sprawling metropolis with a population of over 7.5 million people. But London is also full of beautiful green spaces, with Royal Parks, secret squares and the river offering plenty of chances to escape the hustle and bustle. All this open space also gives you plenty of chances to engage in great sporting activities, whether swimming outdoors or ice skating. But if you'd rather watch the professionals we've also nominated some spectacular sporting events.

*Breathtaking !*

# Beautiful Views

When you're stuck on a packed train or fighting your way through crowds on a busy street, it can be easy to forget what a beautiful city London is. Take some time to admire these favourite views and discover a new appreciation for the city.

### From the Observatory in Greenwich Park

*Greenwich Park, SE10 8QY*
Offering an incredible view of the river Thames and the City of London, including Canary Wharf, it's well worth a trip to the Observatory – you can check out the Prime Meridian line while you're there!

### From King Henry's Mound in Richmond Park

*Richmond Park, TW10 5HS*
The outlook from King Henry's Mound in Richmond Park is a protected view, which means you can see all the way across London to St Paul's. Absolutely spectacular 365 days of the year: autumn, winter, spring or summer, you

Greenwich Park

## From the portico at the entrance to the National Gallery looking south across Trafalgar Square to Big Ben

*Trafalgar Square, WC2N 5DN*

Perfect for a photograph of some iconic London landmarks.

## From the Blue Bridge over the lake in the centre of St James's Park

*St James's Park, SW1A*

Face either Buckingham Palace or Westminster for quintessentially British views. On a sunny day you can hire a deckchair or lounge around on the grass and enjoy the sights. Feels surprisingly countrified.

are guaranteed a beautiful view of the Thames, Twick-enham Stadium and the distant London skyline – and it's free!

## From Primrose Hill on a summer's evening

*Primrose Hill, NW1*

The chance to see an iconic London skyline – you can see the London Eye, the Gherkin, the Zoo, everything! On a sunny day there's a lovely atmosphere as everyone admires the view.

## Walking over one of the city's bridges at night

Whether you walk across the Millennium Bridge, Waterloo, Putney or Hammersmith Bridge, the views of the city lit up at night are incredible when seen reflected in the Thames.

## From Vertigo 42, Top of Tower 42

*Bank, EC2N 1HQ*

Much better views of historic London than the Eye and you also get to drink champagne!

**Tip**

Sitting having a beer at sunset at the Angel pub in Bermondsey, watching the sun set beyond Tower Bridge is the perfect way to end a day in London.

## From Parliament Hill

*Hampstead Heath, NW3*

From the height of Parliament Hill (from where it is rumoured Guy Fawkes had intended to watch the Houses of Parliament explode) you can enjoy a stunning view of the city, truly enjoying its size and spending time identifying the different landmarks.

## SIMPLY SPECTACULAR

# Idyllic Ice Skating

**Even if you're no Torvill and Dean there's nothing that gets you in a festive mood like gliding around an ice rink. Here's our pick of some very special places to go ice skating.**

### Natural History Museum
*South Kensington, SW7 5BD*
Skating in front of the Natural History Museum is always popular and it's a fantastic setting – you can admire the museum all lit up as you make your way around the ice.

### Alexandra Palace
*Muswell Hill, N22 7AY*
This indoor rink has recently undergone a multi-million pound renovation, so it will be in top form. Once you've finished your stint on the ice you can admire the great views of the city.

### Tower of London
*Tower Hill, EC3N 4AB*
Where else will you have the chance to skate in the dry moat of a 900-year-old castle? It can be busy, but the atmospheric backdrop of the tower lit up at night makes this a truly special London experience. There's also a bar serving mulled wine and hot chocolate if you want to take a break.

### Hampton Court
*Hampton Court, KT8 9AU*
Skating at Hampton Court is not only a great festive experience, but it also gives you the chance to admire the beautiful

Ice skating at the Tower of London

architecture of Henry VIII's palace. Make sure to take the time to look around the grounds of the palace as well as gliding around the rink.

Tip
For a contrast to the historical grandeur of skating at this Tudor palace try skating under the thoroughly modern structure of the London Eye.

66 If you're a confident skater the Tower of London is a good place to go on a date! 99

# Urban Oases
# Secret Gardens and Pretty Squares

### Kyoto Garden
*Holland Park*
A peaceful Japanese garden with a pond and waterfall and some seating, making for a pretty place to stop and reflect.

### Inner Temple Gardens
*Holborn, EC4Y 7HL*
Shakespeare set the opening of *Henry VI Part I* in this three-acre garden located next to the Inner Temple, one of the Inns of Court. Open to the public between 12.30pm and 3pm each day, it's a lovely spot to have lunch.

### Geffrye Museum Gardens
*Shoreditch, E2 8EA*
Secluded from the hectic Kingsland Road, this lovely museum has several gardens, including a herb garden and various period gardens.

**Tip**
If you're looking to explore the private gardens in London, go along to the Open Garden Squares Weekend, which takes place at various locations throughout the city in the summer (www.opensquares.org).

### Cleaver Square
*Kennington, SE11 4EA*
A completely unexpected beautiful square in Kennington where you can drink beer and play pétanque on sunny afternoons.

" Neal's Yard is a colourful little refuge of shops and cafes if you need a break from nearby Covent Garden. "

### Russell Square
*Camden, WC1B*
Located near the British Museum, Russell Square is a lovely green space to enjoy a picnic lunch before or after visiting the museum.

### Bloomsbury Square
*Camden, WC1A 2LP*
An oasis of calm in the midst of the bustling centre, the surroundings are fantastic and well worth a visit, or even just a sit down on a busy day in town.

# Let's Go Fly a Kite

### Alexandra Palace
*Muswell Hill, N22 7AY*
High enough to offer good winds, there are great views over London; and it's not as busy as places like Primrose Hill.

### Blackheath
*Blackheath, SE3*
Whatever the weather you're guaranteed big winds and the views are always stunning. There are also lots of nice pubs lining the heath where you can go for a well-deserved drink after your exertions. The Prince's Head is particularly good.

### Parliament Hill, Hampstead Heath
*Hampstead, NW3*
Parliament Hill is approximately 98m (320ft) high, so you're very likely to get a good breeze. Not only do you have a good chance of getting your kite soaring through the air but you'll also be able to enjoy the protected view of the city.

### Streatham Common
*Streatham, SW16*
Streatham Common is a great open space to get a kite flying and once a year it plays host to the Streatham Common Annual Kite Day. There are loads of  kite flying displays as well as music, food and fun for kids.

# Give It a Try

# Fun Places to Watch Six Nations Rugby

### Faltering Fullback Pub
*Finsbury Park, N4 3HB*
There are lots of indoor picnic benches to sit at, the staff are friendly, there are lots of screens to watch the rugby and – most important – the place is full of genuine rugby fans.

### The Underdog
*Clapham Common, SW4 7AB and Northcote Road, SW11 1NT*
There's usually a mixed crowd, making for a great atmosphere, and even when it's rammed, the staff do table service for drinks, so you don't need to miss any of the action waiting at the bar.

# Pack the Hamper
# Perfect Picnic Spots

### Primrose Hill
*Primrose Hill, NW1*
It's a beautiful summer's day, and you want to chill out with a picnic. Grab your hamper and head to the top of Primrose Hill. Spread out your blanket, your crisps and bottles of beer, and let London – from the dome of St Paul's to the gleam of the London Eye – be your ever-inspiring backdrop.

### Wandsworth Park
*Wandsworth, SW15*
A great place for a picnic. Walk along the tree-lined path looking out on the Thames and back towards Putney Bridge before settling down for some food.

### Holland Park
*Holland Park, W8*
Stock up on tasty treats from the Whole Foods Market and then find a nice spot to sit and enjoy them. Holland Park has a mix of open spaces, manicured gardens and areas left in a more natural state. There is also a children's playground if you have little ones who need to burn off some energy.

### Fulham Palace
*Fulham, SW6 6EA*
Situated in Bishop's Park, the grounds of Fulham Palace are an idyllic place to enjoy a picnic. You would never know you're so close to the busy traffic of Putney Bridge as you sit on the grass admiring the architecture of the former home of the bishops of London. If you don't want to bring your own picnic, there's a café where you can buy sandwiches and cakes, and in the summer there's normally a tent with a barbecue and Pimm's on offer. The spot is popular with families with children as the walled garden provides a safe haven for kids to run about.

**Tip**
A smaller alternative to Richmond Park, Richmond Green is a lovely spot in the sun where you can enjoy the beautiful buildings surrounding the green and a drink from one of the neighbouring pubs.

### Phoenix Gardens
*Tottenham Court Road, WC2H 8DG*
A community garden near Tottenham Court Road, this place is a quiet oasis in the middle of the city. It's perfect for a relaxing picnic lunch, and you can even hire the garden if you have a special event coming up.

Picnicking at Primrose Hill

83

## GOING FOR GOLD

# Spectacular Sporting Events

## Must-See

### London Marathon

On one Sunday in April London goes running mad. Go along to take in the action and cheer on the runners – the atmosphere anywhere along the route is electric. It's best to watch this event along the north bank of the Thames between the 25th and 26th mile. It's also a great way to spot celebs!

### Oxford and Cambridge Boat Race

Held every year in late March/early April, the rowing race between Oxford and Cambridge brings over 200,000 people to the banks of the river between Putney and Mortlake. You can watch the start at Putney Bridge or the end at Chiswick Bridge, but one of the best places to watch the race is just by Hammersmith Bridge in Furnival Gardens. It's a small green space and does get busy, though less so than the Putney launch. It also has a lot of food and drink stalls.

> " Watching the runners and thinking about all the money being raised for charity really inspires me and makes me a bit emotional! "

### Matches at one of London's football clubs

London is home to some of the best football teams in Europe: there are the Premier League greats Arsenal, Chelsea and Tottenham, and smaller clubs like Fulham and Crystal Palace, which also have an incredible atmosphere and offer quality football. If you visit Fulham, take time to admire the Johnny Haynes Stand which is Grade II listed and the oldest football stand in the world.

### Wimbledon

Whether you're cheering on the latest British hopeful or eating strawberries and cream, a trip to Wimbledon is brilliant fun. You can apply for public ballot tickets or you can just turn up and join what must be the ultimate British queue. The queue is an amazing experience; there's a good atmosphere while you're waiting, with tennis facts posted along the way and local residents selling food from their driveways. If you can get there on a weekday (especially in the first week when more tennis is played), and only have a ground pass, it's well worth waiting until the end of the day inside the

*Tip*

It's £5 for the shuttle bus from Wimbledon station, but also a £5 flat fare in a taxi from the same place!

grounds, as this is when they re-sell the returned tickets for the show courts for a £10 donation to charity. You can see some amazing matches with the top seeded players.

## Alternative Sporting Events

### ■ Tree-Athlon

The Tree-Athlon is a 5km race through Battersea Park which aims to raise money to plant trees in cities and help make urban areas more green. At the end of the race there's live music, games, face painting and even a world record attempt!

### ■ Army vs Navy rugby

A fierce competition, played since 1920, culminating in a final match played at Twickenham for the Babcock Trophy. The rivalry between the two sides is intense, guaranteeing a passionate crowd and an energetic game.

### ■ Great River Race

A 21-mile charity race from Millwall to Richmond, the Great River Race features 300 boats and 2,000 competitors, many in fancy dress, battling it out for a range of prizes. There's a real variety of vessels involved, from Viking longboats to Chinese dragon boats. You can watch from a few places, but you'll get a good view of the colourful display from one of the bridges on the route, such as Westminster Bridge or Kew Bridge.

### ■ ATP World Finals

The ATP Finals, held at the O2 Arena, is not your typical tennis tournament. The atmosphere and venue are very different from the formality and tradition of Wimbledon, but the music, lights and smoke effects all combine to give an electric feel and the round-robin format gives you a great chance to see the top eight players battle it out for the title.

Some of the 300 boats in the Great River Race

# Royal Salute

# Places or Events Where You Can See the Queen

**If it doesn't look as if you're going to get an invite to the Garden Party at Buckingham Palace this year, why not pop along to one of these events to get a glimpse of the Queen as she goes about her official duties.**

## ▮ Trooping the Colour

In celebration of the Queen's official birthday in June a military parade is held at Horse Guards Parade. The Queen travels from Buckingham Palace to Horse Guards Parade, where she is presented with the colours and flags of the Guards regiments. It's a wonderful spectacle and a great example of British pomp and circumstance. You can apply for tickets to watch from the seated stands by writing to Brigade Major, HQ Household Division, Horse Guards, Whitehall, London, SW1A 2AX. You can also apply for tickets for the rehearsal a week before or watch the procession from the Mall.

## ▮ State Opening of Parliament

The formal opening of a new session of Parliament sees the Queen in all her

finery in the grand setting of the Houses of Parliament. The Queen gives a speech setting out the government's business for that year after travelling in the Irish state coach from Buckingham Palace. The parade includes a guard of honour and the Household Cavalry. You can watch the procession from the Mall or Whitehall, but one of the best spots is next to the House of Lords in St Margaret's Street. This event also gives you the chance to see the Imperial State Crown as it travels in front of the Queen in a state coach of its own.

## ▮ Garter Day service

The Garter Day service is held to celebrate the Knights of the Order of the Garter, the oldest and most senior order of chivalry in England. After the ceremony at Windsor Castle (where new knights are invested) the Queen, royal family and knights proceed to St George's Chapel. You can apply for tickets to watch the procession by emailing garterday.info@royal.gsx.gov.uk.

Trooping the Colour

## WHEN YOU NEED AN ESCAPE

# Beautiful
# Green Spaces

**If you're not lucky enough to have your own garden or you're looking for a place to play some impromptu football or Frisbee, head to one of London's many parks.**

### ■ Greenwich Park
*Greenwich, SE10*
The oldest park in London, Greenwich Park is a lovely place to visit after a day exploring maritime Greenwich. With great views over London and a children's playground, it's an idyllic spot.

### ■ Richmond Park
*Richmond, TW10 5HS*
The best of the former hunting estates that shows absolute balance between perfect wilderness and parkland. It's a huge park (2,500 acres) and is home to nearly 700 deer that wander freely through the park.

### ■ Clapham Common
*Clapham, SW4*
A vast green space with a lot of amenities nearby. It's great to visit on a sunny

Clapham Common

day and maybe grab some dinner or a drink from one of the nearby pubs and restaurants.

### ■ St James's Park
*St James's Park, SW1A*
Originally a hunting ground for Henry VIII, St James's Park is the smallest park in central London. Home to Buckingham Palace, the Mall and Horse Guards Parade, this is a great royal London spot. Relax in a deck chair and listen to a free concet at the band stand in summer.

### ■ Wimbledon Common
*Wimbledon, SW19*
The common land made up of Wimbledon Common, Putney Heath and

Deer in Richmond Park

Deck chairs at Green Park

Putney Common offers 1,140 acres of wild land to enjoy. Parts of the common are areas of special scientific interest and are home to a variety of flora and fauna.

### Green Park
*Piccadilly, W1J*

Green Park supposedly got its name because the wife of Charles II stopped flowers being planted so her husband couldn't give them to his many mistresses. Today, though, Green Park is full of colourful flowers and in the summer you can hire a deckchair.

### Bishop's Park
*Fulham, SW6*

A fantastic location for a walk along the river on a sunny day, particularly during the summer months when it is

Along the Serpentine, Hyde Park

full of dogs! You can also visit the lovely café in Fulham Palace for a bite to eat.

### Hyde Park
*Mayfair, W2*

A Royal Park which is great for cycling or hiring boats on the Serpentine Lake. This is also the home of the Princess Diana Memorial Fountain, which is a lovely spot to visit on a hot day.

### Bushy Park
*Teddington, TW11*

This historical Royal Park is close to Hampton Court Palace and contains beautiful water gardens. There are also a number of deer wandering freely through the park.

Chestnut Avenue, Bushy Park

### Battersea Park
*Battersea, SW11*

Located next to the Thames across from Chelsea, Battersea Park has a great children's zoo as well as all-weather sports pitches.

### Potters Field Park
*Southwark, SE1 3JB*

Gorgeous space in the heart of the city with views of Tower Bridge and the Tower of London.

Kensington Gardens

## Regent's Park
*Camden, NW1*
One of the larger Royal Parks, Regent's Park is home to London Zoo and is the venue for several sporting events. There's also an open-air theatre during the summer.

## Kensington Gardens
*Kensington, W2*
Home to the famous Peter Pan statue, Kensington Gardens is immediately adjacent to Hyde Park and is a lovely place to relax after a visit to Kensington Palace.

**Tip**
Hire a deckchair in one of the Royal Parks for a really chilled-out time in the sun.

## Victoria Park
*Hackney, E9*
London's first public park, 'Vicky Park' is a large green space which is often the venue for music festivals.

## Holland Park
*Kensington, W8*
This parkland in upmarket Chelsea is considered to be one of the most romantic parks in London, with its woodland, wildlife and the Kyoto Japanese Garden. It's also home to opera in the summer.

## Crystal Palace Park
*Crystal Palace, SE19*
The only park in London with resident dinosaurs – kids love searching for the full-size sculptures of the prehistoric creatures. There's also a playground and a good exhibition at the site of the Crystal Palace itself.

## Hampstead Heath
*Hampstead, NW3*
This is nearly 800 acres of wild landscape. A contrast to more manicured parks, Hampstead Heath is a wonderful place to explore and admire the view from Parliament Hill down to Canary Wharf.

## Ravenscourt Park
*Hammersmith, W6*
With playgrounds, a basketball court, a bowling green and a sandpit there's something fun for everyone in this lesser-known park.

## Brockwell Park
*Herne Hill, SE24*
With a lido, miniature railway, a BMX track and wonderful views of the City skyline, Brockwell is a great family park and is also home to the Lambeth Country Show each summer.

# Wish You Were Here
# Fun Things to Do with Visitors

Anyone who lives in London will soon discover the fear that grips you when you have people coming to stay: 'What am I going to do with them?!' You want to do something uniquely London but not too clichéd. Here are our top choices for some fun things to do with visitors that you'll really enjoy as well.

London Duck Tours

### ■ London Duck Tours
*Departs near Waterloo, SE1 7PY*
Better than a boat tour or open top bus tour, a duck tour combines both! Setting out in an amphibious vehicle, you drive into the river (quite a hair-raising moment!) before being given a guided tour of London's famous river sights including a great view of the Houses of Parliament. Loads of fun, even for long-term London residents.

### ■ Kew Gardens
*Richmond, TW9*
Wonderfully pretty gardens with a lake, greenhouses, a treetop walk, music nights, cafés and lots of grassy areas where you can sit and have a picnic. There can be a queue on a hot summer's day, but it's well worth it!

### ■ Dennis Severs' House
*Spital fields, E1 6BX*
One of London's quirkier 'museums', it contains 10 rooms recreating life in the area in the 18th and 19th centuries,

Drawing Room of Dennis Severs' House

down to the smells and sounds. The attention to detail is awesome; it really feels like stepping back in time.

## Football stadium tours
*Various locations*
If you know any football fans, a visit to one of the capital's football stadiums can be a real treat. You can go for a tour of Wembley to relive some of English football's famous moments or visit the home of one of the super clubs, such as Arsenal's Emirates Stadium. A slightly cheaper option can be a smaller club like Fulham, which has listed turnstiles and is London's oldest professional football club.

# Odd Street Names

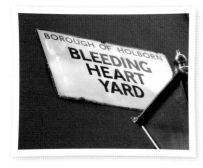

- Frying Pan Alley, E1
- Anne of Cleeves Close, SE9
- St Mary Axe, EC3A
- Kitcat Terrace, E3
- Man in Moon Passage, W1
- Cinderella Path, NW1
- Bleeding Heart Yard, EC1N
- Ha-ha Road, SE18
- Ave Maria Lane, EC4
- Shoulder of Mutton Alley, E14
- Quaggy Walk, SE3

- Czar Street, SE8
- Ogle Street, W1W
- Elvis Road, NW2
- Hanging Sword Alley, EC4
- Dog Kennel Hill, SE22
- Giant Tree Hill, WD23
- Little Britain, EC1A
- Tweezers Alley, WC2R
- Peppermint Place, E11
- Electric Avenue, SW9
- Cyclops Mews, E14
- Hen and Chicken Court, EC4

# Wonderful Walks

**Going for a walk in London is a fantastic way to learn how all the individual and unique areas that make up the city's character link together. Here are our top routes.**

### Along Regent's Canal

A gorgeous winding canal walk, passing Broadway Market, lots of canal boats and plenty of cute little coffee shops and pubs en route.
Perfect for a sunny spring afternoon! You can stop by Camden Lock to browse the stalls and continue on to Little Venice to enjoy the bars and cafés.

### From the South Bank (Royal Festival Hall) to Tower Hill

This is an excellent urban riverside walk. On the way you will pass such iconic landmarks as the Globe theatre, the Oxo Tower and City Hall. And there's a marina at Tower Hill which is pleasant to amble around.

### The Strand on the Green (Chiswick)

A stretch of the shore on the north side of the Thames downstream from Kew Bridge, the views are ever-changing due to the variations in the light on the river. It is normally very peaceful, except for warm summer weekends when it can be busy. There are three pubs – the Bell and Crown, City Barge and the Bull – where you can enjoy a drink and some food. Be aware that at some high tides the path will flood for a short time so you might get wet feet while having a drink!

**Tip**

If you're looking for reliable routes for London walks look at the Pathfinder Guide *London's Parks and Countryside*. You could also check out guided tours by London Walks (www.walks.com) and the Blood and Tears Walk (www.shockinglondon.com).

### Wimbledon Common

There are several routes you can take through the expansive Wimbledon Common, but a particularly pleasant walk takes you from Putney Heath to Wimbledon Village.

### Hampstead Heath

The 800 acres of Hampstead Heath provide numerous routes, but some key places you should make sure to see are Parliament Hill (the view is amazing) and Kenwood House, an 18th-century Robert Adam country house.
There are also some great pubs, like Jack Straw's Castle, where you can stop and have a rest.

# River Antics
# Fun on the Thames

### Boating

There are several places you can hire boats in London: the Royal Parks, Hyde Park and Regent's Park hire out rowing boats, while at Battersea Park you can row or pedal your way around the lake. One of the most picturesque places to hire a boat is Richmond, where you can hire a rowing boat and explore the river or the lake in Richmond Park.

### Walking along the riverside

A walk along any part of the riverside encompasses the beauty and calm of the Thames. Whether it's along the South Bank opposite the House of Parliament or the quiet greenery between Richmond and Kew, a walk along the riverside is really special.

### Enjoying a drink on the riverside

Some of London's best pubs are on the river, especially out east. It's a real London experience to be next to the river, drink in hand, admiring one of the many great views that these riverside pubs have to offer.

**Tip**
Try the Prospect of Whitby for a great spot on the Thames.

### Boat trips in central London

Several tour companies offer a tour of the Thames and it's a great way to see London landmarks. Even if you don't want to go on an organised tour you can catch the Thames Clipper between the Tate museums or from the O2 Arena to Waterloo.

### Bridges

Walk over any of London's many bridges, from historic Richmond Bridge to the new Millennium Bridge, and you'll get a brilliant view of the Thames and how it snakes through the city.

### Canal boats

If you're feeling like a real adventure on the water, why not hire a canal boat? Several companies offer hire and some even do dinner cruises and tours. The London Canal Museum runs a variety of tours, including a Hallowe'en tour!

Boating Lake, Richmond

## PLACES TO MAKE A SPLASH!

# Top Swimming Pools

### Hampstead Lido

*On the foot of Hampstead Heath, north west London*

The pool is massive (50m long), clean and well-kept and is great for an open air swim and a dip to keep cool in the summer.

### Pools on the Park

*Richmond, TW9 2SL*

Pools on the Park is a great swimming pool for both fitness and fun. It has a large indoor and outdoor pool (during the summer months), which is extremely popular. The indoor pool is great for fitness and lane swimming, and the outdoor pool is perfect for a more leisurely swim and, if you're lucky, a suntan. Be warned that the outdoor pool does get very busy in school holidays.

### Marshall Street Leisure Centre

*Soho, W1F 7EL*

Enjoy a dip in the heart of London, at this magnificent 1930s, marble lined pool. The Grade II listed building recently re-opened after extensive redevelopment.

### Oasis, Endell Street

*Covent Garden, WC2H 9AG*

The outdoor pool at this centrally located sports centre is great on a sunny day and there's even a sun terrace if you want to soak up some rays. You can pay a one-off fee to use the pool if you're not a member.

### Tooting Bec Lido

*Tooting Bec, SW16 1RU*

This lido has won awards as the best open-air swimming pool in London and as it's one of the biggest (twice the length of an Olympic swimming pool) it's a great place for everyone to swim peacefully and uninterrupted.

Tooting Bec Lido

### London Fields Lido

*Hackney, E8 3EU*

An Olympic-sized, heated outdoor pool, this is a great place to cool off on a hot day.

Tip

Try out the Serpentine Lido in the middle of Hyde Park – it's a freshwater lido and so doesn't have any chlorine in the water.

# Area Index

## Our Wonderful Contributors

Our thanks go to all of the Londoners who took time to give us their fabulous recommendations and tips. In particular we would like to thank:

Ethan Orwin, Amy Rose, Andrew Smith, Georgina-Kate Adams, James Campbell, Sophie Hannon, Gavin Webb (www.tourguideoflondon.co.uk), Esther Batterbee, Gary Wayment, Lucy Smith, Lauren Blackwell, Nick Clarke, Rebecca Ramsay, David Ainsworth, Beth Bishop, Susannah Lear, Cormac Byrne, Maggie Smith, Rebecca Brett, Cory Santos, Simon Connor, Shivani Shah, David Clark, Jo Jacomb, Hatty Aldridge, Jake Fieller, Anthea Ross, Jonny Young, Catherine Porritt, Robin Boothroyd, Rachel Pearce, Jack Donaldson, Hugh Brune, Lucy Edmonds, Joe Williams, Anna Williamson, William Sumners, Cara Cahill, Graham Walden, Sally Pitts, Chris Thomas, Lizzie Rafii-Tabar, Rich Paylor, Teresa Paddington, Ian Bloodworth, Sophie Thomas, Anton Panchenkov, Jane Parker, Caroline Maddison, Flora Tonking (The Accidental Londoner, http://theaccidentallondoner.blogspot.com), Libby Walden, Sarah Wasser, Laura Emily White, Clare Blanchfield, Lucy Elizabeth Smith, Karen Orwin, Jess Latapie, Jessica Spencer, Laura Porter (golondon.about.com).

Richmond Green